ELIZABETH GRANT

MY LIFE—MY STORY

Written by

Marion Suzenne Witz
& Carol Krenz

authorHOUSE®

AuthorHouse™
1663 Liberty Drive
Bloomington, IN 47403
www.authorhouse.com
Phone: 1-800-839-8640

First published by AuthorHouse 11/30/2009

ISBN: 978-1-4490-4762-7 (e)
ISBN: 978-1-4490-4760-3 (sc)
ISBN: 978-1-4490-4761-0 (hc)

Library of Congress Control Number: 2009912968

Printed in the United States of America
Bloomington, Indiana

This book is printed on acid-free paper.

DEDICATION

I dedicate this book to all women who have said "I can't, I'm too tall, too short, too fat, too thin, too plain, too ..."

To you I say, "Yes you can."

You can be whoever you want to be.

I also dedicate this book to me beloved Papa, who always guided me and helped me and loves me to this very day.

FOREWORD

Marion Suzenne Witz (a.k.a. Suzenne Best)

I'll never forget the day I met Elizabeth. Of course, I was nervous — who wouldn't be? I knew that she was a powerhouse, dynamic, very beautiful, and extremely successful. "She shoots it straight from the hip," I was told. "Make sure you look your best, don't slouch in the chair, stop licking your lips, *and don't* chew gum. Elizabeth notices *everything* ..."

Everything? Oh dear. I wasn't sophisticated. I never bothered about dressing well. I was a girl next door, wearing basic jeans, sneakers, and T-shirts—casual and always comfortable. I lived a very average life where not much happened. I didn't think there was anything wrong with the way I looked, but after I heard this, I started to fret. Dressing for Elizabeth became an obsession; I wanted to look perfect. I went to the hairdresser, and of course, he cut my hair too short. I went shopping for the perfect outfit and felt like a frump. And the shoes …

The shoes I purchased (after the salesgirl told me that they were *absolutely perfect*) were too high, too clumpy, and … *white.* "You bought white shoes! How many times have I told you that Elizabeth always says, 'White shoes are for brides and tennis players'?" This was going to be a disaster. Naturally, the white shoes went to the back of my closet and I started again. This time I paged through catalogues and started to look for the right look

In a nutshell, when I met Elizabeth I got everything wrong but meeting her made everything right. As I approached her, she turned around, her face lit up with a warm, sunny glow, and she said, "Marion, I'm so glad to finally meet you. You are more than everything I imagined." She put her arm around me and made me feel as though I was the most important person she had ever met. It didn't matter what I was wearing or how I looked. What mattered most was that we were now together and had a lot of catching up to do.

Although I didn't start to work with Elizabeth until years later, the first time we met in Canada has always remained one of those memories that as I think about it, I smile, because the day I met Elizabeth was the beginning of a life-changing adventure that still continues.

I had been married to Paul, Elizabeth's son, for twelve years. We were living with our three children in Canada, and although we regularly received chatty letters and care parcels from Elizabeth about what was happening in South Africa, who got married, had a party, what was on sale, the latest gossip—very newsy tidbits on life back home—we had never actually met, and this was why it was a big deal for me. The care parcels were always loads of fun for the family when they arrived. Elizabeth made sure that everyone got something—chocolates for Paul; comics, books, toys, and stylish clothes for the children; and Elizabeth Grant skincare for me. Honestly, I was not impressed with my "gifts." I shoved them in the back of the cupboard or gave them away. In my own little way, I was inadvertently building a loyal following of Torricelumn girls because my friends and family repeatedly asked me for more of *that stuff*," but at the time this was not my intention. I was a "brand snob"—nothing but a big brand label was good enough for me and my mother-in-law's stuff didn't cut it. Years later I realized how foolish this was, and today (having used Elizabeth Grant for over ten years) I bless Elizabeth every time I look in the mirror.

Mother-in-law—daughter-in-law. At first I thought I was lucky that my mother-in-law lived on a different continent. My friends constantly complained that their mother-in-law interfered, passed comments, or gave them "the look." I didn't have these issues. I put it down to the fact that we lived in different countries, but this really was not the case. When Elizabeth and I first spoke on the phone she said, "You are the mother of my grandchildren, the wife of my son. I will never have a fight with you." And she never has. You see, when Elizabeth gives her word, it is cast in stone.

Our relationship has grown from mother-in-law and daughter-in-law to a true friendship. When we first went on air together I was so shy I used my middle name, Suzenne. I needed a last name and Elizabeth sweetly quipped – "Suzenne, in my mind you're the best so from now on your name is Suzenne Best.

I respect, trust, and love Elizabeth and enjoy sharing my life with her. We have travelled all over the world together. We laugh a lot. We shop, dine, watch movies, go to the theater, and when it comes to business, seek out each other's opinion and then move forward. Elizabeth is , stylish, a fashion icon, witty, and very smart. She is what every woman aspires to be, and I am fortunate to be part of her family.

I know that I wouldn't be where I am today if it were not for Elizabeth. She has taught me courage, independence, self-reliance, and the essence of being a woman. She has also taught me to become aware of my own inner beauty, and today I feel I shine. I know of so many people who Elizabeth has touched in the same way.

While working on the book, Elizabeth shared many experiences with me that were impactful, and after our conversations, I would find myself thinking very deeply about how she was able to mold herself into the person she became through conscious effort. I learned that it is not luck that makes you who you are but the effort you put into yourself, and I learned from Elizabeth that the true secret to success is hard work and commitment.

Elizabeth's message is one of hope, of how to overcome adversity through drive and determination. Elizabeth's life was fraught with so much suffering. Many a time when she had just started an upward climb, something, someone, or some event would knock her sideways. But because she knew what she wanted from life, she never let these obstacles deter her vision, which is why today she can look back at her life and say, "I made it!"

Marion Witz, President of Elizabeth Grant International Inc, is based out of Toronto, Canada. Marion has authored, *Stand Up and Talk to 1000 People (And Enjoy It!)*, helping readers empower their voice and strengthen their expression.   In May 2006, Marion was selected by the City of Toronto to be a part of the city wide poster campaign, *We Build This City*, which recognized the experiences of Toronto's most talented and skilled business leaders. She is considered one of Canada's top women entrepreneurs, having been recognized on the Profit W100's ranking for last four consecutive years.

PROLOGUE

─────── ❀ ───────

CAROL KRENZ

I discovered Elizabeth Grant the way thousands of people do. I was flipping through myriad television programmes and landed at The Shopping Channel in Canada when she was presenting her skin-care line. I sat up immediately. Here was a uniquely charismatic woman of intense passion and zest selling out individual products almost as fast as she could introduce them.

I was greatly impressed. As a beauty journalist for more than twenty years, I had sampled them all—thousands of lotions and creams promising the world, delivering little, and in some cases, costing as much as the gross national product of Luxemburg. I confess I am a beauty junkie but one who is infused with healthy skepticism.

I was not prepared for Elizabeth's unique style. She was speaking so earnestly, so charmingly. She was completely disarming. Silver-haired and a self-proclaimed octogenarian, she stood a scant few inches above five feet, sporting a square-neck top that revealed a smooth and creamy décolleté. Her cupid mouth wore a luxurious shade of red, and her luminous complexion leapt right through the cameras. Matching this striking image was her voice, rich and melodious in an English accent that tilted from authoritative received pronunciation to the humour of the Midlands. Her brown eyes, dark, large, and intense, brimmed with emotion as her words poured forth with endless zeal and wit.

"Be a clever girl," she was advising, "and stock up! At this price you'll kick yourself if you don't. It's got a shelf life of three years, and you'll be set for the season."

I do not recall what the product was. It might have been her now-famous serum or a package of numerous products grouped as the daily showstopper, but it doesn't matter. The point was, I had discovered her, and like thousands of other viewers, try as I might, I simply could not *stop* watching her.

Why? What was it about this woman that was so compelling? I stayed with her shows for the rest of the day and snapped up almost everything she had to offer. What's more, I endorse her line as the most splendid and effective I have ever used. But the magic of her products is really beside the point. And that's why this book had to be.

What captured me about Elizabeth's on-air persona was the way she shared intimate bits and pieces of her life. Personal stories and anecdotal quips peppered her speech. Her entire raison d'être about the magnificence of Torricelumn™—the cornerstone marine ingredient of all her anti-aging lines—lay in the reality of wartime London and a bomb blast whose flying debris hit the left side of her face and neck, badly scarring her, just missing her eye, and leaving her permanently deaf in the left ear. It was a tragedy, she said, that changed her life completely.

She talked about working as a makeup artist in various London film studios peopled by such twentieth-century luminaries as Vivien Leigh, Robert Taylor, Laurence Olivier, Margaret Lockwood, Claire Trevor, Margaret Leighton, and more. Trying to carry on in that environment with facial scarring was next to impossible. She felt horribly deformed, embarrassed, and thought life as she knew it was over.

Often she lapsed into advice from her mother, who had lived to 104. She elaborated on her own personal bath and beauty rituals and joked about life at home with a little dog: "He's blind and I'm deaf. We make quite a pair!"

The more she talked, the more I wanted to listen. It occurred to me that her charming stories and memories provoke a hunger in anyone who's ever longed for a grandmother, or an audaciously witty aunt. There was a universality to her approach, an enormous warmth and mothering that coloured her views on age, women, and the art of beauty. "Mother Nature," she declared, "is not on your side. But I am!"

Then there was another more formidable aspect of Elizabeth Grant. She was unquestionably an indefatigable woman who simply refused to sit still on a rapidly expanding global empire and enjoy well-deserved leisure. On the surface, she gave one to believe that her life was entirely about skincare and anti-aging. But darting in and around her fabulous products lurked another depth of living and a philosophy that could not be ignored.

By day's end, I knew I had to speak with her and with anyone who could shed more light on her. It has taken me several years to get here, but every step has been worth it.

Elizabeth Grant is mercurial and enigmatic. Although initially private and protective of certain events in her life—and who wouldn't be?—she offers important glimpses into the spectrum of human existence. Anxious that her legion of "Torricelumn girls" not think she was born with a silver spoon in her mouth, and aware that everyone wants a memento, a legacy in writing, she consented at last to the book. She doesn't want it to be about her crowning achievements and beauty advice, although they do inevitably seep in. Rather, her conversations and stories serve to illustrate the importance of human perseverance.

Marion and I spent many hours compiling this book. Initially I wanted to tell the story of Elizabeth's life—her history—and then with Marion's help I realized that this book would be so much more. I began reviewing Elizabeth's formative years, a study in contrasts. Many of them, I thought, were unspeakably depressing and brutal, but when I tiptoed into this conversation with Elizabeth, she smiled at me and said, "You know, Carol, life is how you make it. I have learned that no matter how bleak a situation is there's always a light out there waiting. I look back at my life and realize that I have been blessed because somehow I always found the light. Sometimes it was a faint glimmer and other times a bright flash, but it was always there waiting for me." I soon realized that my sessions with Elizabeth would be more than just her life story.

Our talks began over the phone in the fall of 2008—Elizabeth in Toronto and me in Montreal. Tentative at first, Elizabeth gradually warmed to the idea of revealing more than perhaps she initially intended, and I thank her for this privilege. Elizabeth is a very private, good person. My intention with this book was never to dwell on the negative as, "The past is the past—it can't be changed. Only we can change and determine what we want to accomplish with our lives," as Elizabeth would say. When Elizabeth let things drop in bits and bobs, a tuppence here, a farthing there, I scrambled to scoop them up. Dusted off and brightly polished, they provided the cornerstones of her life. Some of these remarkable coins would be better off tossed overboard at sea. But that would not do the truth of Elizabeth Grant any justice. What she has accomplished despite enormous odds to the contrary helped me learn and understand that we are all responsible for who we are. This is the message that I hope permeates my book. The essence of Elizabeth Grant is a journey of self-empowerment.

Our conversations, regardless of the subject, always included a parting joke from her seemingly endless collection, because humour is one of Elizabeth's strongest motivators. "I absolutely adore making people laugh," she says. Humour is a great equalizer, and she serves it up banquet-style. Elizabeth is droll, acerbic, witty, bawdy, a born mimic with a dollop of drama. She pokes fun at life and at herself.

"Everyone knows me at the mall," she recounted one afternoon. "Probably because (and I shouldn't admit this) I'm there so often. I love going into the stores. My favourites are the dress stores and Berani Jewelers. I spend hours with Saro der Haroutiunian discussing his new pieces and together we have created the most beautiful jewelry designs for my Private Collection. Many a time he asks me my opinion, and it's flattering that he's impressed with how much I actually know. I took a course in gemology years ago, and I have an acute ability to grade stones. When I look at a stone, I know the size, the colour, clarity, cut, and quality. Anyway, I'm digressing." Elizabeth often did this, and I have to tell you I loved these digressions, as I learned so much with each story. "Sometimes, I cheer myself up by going for a stroll in the mall to say hi to everyone. One day when I was feeling a little down—it happens to all of us—I said to myself (you know Carol I talk to myself a lot), 'That's enough. *Go out!' I* got all dressed up, threw on a mink, and sailed right over there. It was such a lift to my spirits. People smiled at me and I smiled back. I popped in and out of the shops, and I was feeling very spiffy. I knew I looked glam, so I thought I would spend a bit more time wandering around, and that's just what I did, only this time *I took my time*—popping into shops, smiling back at all the friendly people who were smiling at me. Okay," said Elizabeth, "I may as well get to the end of the story. When I got home, I looked in the mirror, and would you believe it? I had been walking around with two large pink curlers on the top of my head!" Elizabeth burst out laughing and continued, "So there I was feeling very glamourous and gorgeous and all those people who I thought were being friendly were probably looking at me and thinking, *OMG, look at that funny lady with the curlers in her hair.*"

I came to realize there isn't a single aspect of Elizabeth's life that isn't a dichotomy and that she herself is the eternal puzzle wrapped in an enigma. You can speak to her for hours and never know what might bubble to the surface. Her tears are often joyous, and her laughter, once a clever mask for fear and despair, now bubbles to the surface with true merriment and delight. "I have learned to love life, and I treasure every moment."

Shortly after I started work on the book, I flew to Toronto and met with Elizabeth and Marion at the plant, which is large, modern, and very impressive. Our visit was warm and intimate, and I was eager to close the gap between the voice over the phone and the actual person. Elizabeth said I surprised her (which I took to mean she had expected a more *studious-looking* woman). After my first glance I said, "You're gorgeous."

Elizabeth, whose face looked even more radiant in person, was dressed in a butter-soft Italian black leather jacket, a cashmere sweater, and slacks. She appeared ageless—like a beautiful and wise faerie queen who tends roses and catches sunbeams and dewdrops in her delicate palms. But as we sat and sipped coffee side by side in her office, she stretched her legs, crossed them, and shapely ankles shot into view. Very shapely ankles. Faerie-shmaerie! She was sensuous, lithe, and curvaceous—things one cannot notice on television because she's always standing behind a table. She looked like a hottie, and I told her so.

"Don't be silly!" she exclaimed. "What are you going on about? I am an old woman!"

"I don't care what your age is," I insisted. "I'm telling you, you're one sexy mama."

She remained silent. She probably thought I was mad. But I assure you ... she's a hottie.

And the other truth is that she's led one hell of a life. A lesser person would have thrown in the towel at twenty. But Elizabeth, thank heavens, is not that person. She is extraordinarily unique, and this book attempts to explain why.

Carol Krenz is a beauty, fashion and entertainment writer. Her non-fiction books include *Audrey: A Life in Pictures* (a biography of Audrey Hepburn) and *100 Years of Hollywood: A Century of Movie Magic*. She lives in Montreal and is currently at work on fiction.

CHAPTER 1

THE EARLY YEARS: LESSONS IN SELF-RELIANCE

I was born in the early 1900s in London, England. The world was turbulent at the beginning of the twentieth century, caught in the crumbling grasp of Europe's royal dynasties. Revolt and rebellion whispered through political corridors and uncertainty defined the era. In Russia, the Romanov Tsar, Nicholas II, wielded iron power, and within Russia's western provinces, known as the Pale of Settlement, persecution against Jews meant deadly pogroms—state-sanctioned, unprovoked attacks on lives and property. It was from this kind of assault that my mother, Alice, fled, along with her brother and two sisters. She had witnessed local brutality and had watched Cossacks burn her home to the ground.

Armed with considerable wits, she and her siblings headed to England. The rough voyage and subsequent entrance into London was similar to the experience of thousands of other refugees pouring into large cities in both Western Europe and North America. It was the age of the greatest population migration in history, marked by ever-increasing eruptions of war and the rise of new political movements.

In London, Yiddish-speaking organizations such as the Jewish Board of Deputies and the Zionist Federation stationed themselves at the piers, offering the new immigrants immediate help and information.

"When my mother arrived in London, she couldn't speak a word of English. She had no money, no family, and no job. All she owned was what she was could carry and whatever her mother had sewn into her skirt.

Notorious for its Cockney inhabitants, its winding, narrow streets, and the salacious murders of Jack the Ripper, the East End became home to most of the new Jewish immigrants. Many took up the local needle trade, which had begun in the 1700s with Protestant Huguenots fleeing Catholic France. Traces of their elaborate couture shops and princely homes still dotted Brick Lane.

British society was in flux. Queen Victoria died in 1901, but the rigidity of social manners and mores—not to mention the elitist class system—was still very much in place. King Edward VII ushered in the brief Edwardian Age, a final and feeble nod to entrenched nineteenth-century values before the stirrings of modernity and the First World War in 1914 gave everyone—from the manor on down—a resounding shake, collapsing the rigid social structure of the British society. The war elevated the position of women in that women started to work in offices and munitions factories and do what was always termed "men's work." This was the true era of the emancipation of women. It was a time when women started to raise the bar for themselves, giving themselves a new sense of self-worth and a realization of what they were capable and able of achieving. The women in England threw off their Victorian ideals and started to create a new identity and a new place for themselves in society.

Even though it was not easy for a woman to make it independently and even though it was legislated that women would be deployed after the war and their jobs given back to men, once change starts it is almost impossible to go backward. For the first time the definitions of "women's work" and "men's work" was challenged. Politically the women's movement challenged the bill of 1918 that gave women the right to vote only if they were over thirty and ten years later, in 1928 they won. All women over the age of twenty-one were given the right to vote and the right to own property.

For the first time in the history of England (that I know of) women could own their property and vote. This was a huge liberation for women, as before this women were not allowed to have control over their assets; their husband, or if they didn't have a husband, a male relative, was given control over their finances.

One lesson I have learned in life it is that it is absolutely essential for a woman to have access to her own funds. This gives and maintains our independence. If we don't, then we become reliant on the largesse of our husband or partner.

The early 1920s was the age when women took off their corsets and for the first time in centuries showed their legs. This was the age of movies. Fashion was heavily influenced by the newly created larger than life movie stars. Vogue Magazine and Harper's Bazaar gained mass appeal.

How was I influenced by all this? Technically I was too young to understand this new enlightenment, but my mother was certainly the first liberated woman in our family, and this had a profound effect on my life.

My mother embodied the true spirit of this modern woman. She was fiercely independent and never accepted the social restraints of what was the right or wrong way to behave. She had always stood up to anyone and anything with an air of defiance. I rapidly absorbed my mother's examples of fierce independence. One of the most important lessons that continually filtered down was that people will only do to you what you allow them to do. She told me, "You put your own price on your head. I value my life and will not allow others to tell me what I can or should do!"

Soon after arriving in England, she married, gave birth to Ann, and then promptly divorced her husband on a charge of infidelity. Can you imagine the disgrace? In those days it was unheard of for a woman to evict a husband from his home. And to divorce a man was scandalous! But my mother was never one to worry about what other people said; she did what she believed was right for herself.

Scandalous behaviour or not, Mummy met and married her second husband, my father, Morris, who came from Vienna. I was born soon after the end of World War I, the infamous "war to end all wars," which, if anything, only laid the groundwork for an even larger conflagration to come. But no one was thinking about this when the Roaring Twenties arrived. There were new freedoms, unimaginable stock-market prosperity in the United States, greater women's rights, and a cultural revolution in art, fashion, and lifestyle. Calls for free thinkers, decadent Fauvist dancing, and Rudolf Valentino motion pictures whirled about my mother like Coco Chanel's iconic No. 5, but had no bearing on me, who was now taking my first steps in the dreamy mists of a fairytale.

In the beginning, life was good. My father, who I called Papa, owned a very modern and successful blouse factory capable of mass production. We enjoyed great affluence. Papa drove a fashionable, jazz-hot Daimler, and I recall my mother dressed in an elaborate full-length beaded gown that cost a hundred pounds at a time when a loaf of bread was a penny. As in most good homes, there were servants and a nanny.

Mummy had a great zest for life. My mother was strikingly beautiful. She was tall, about five-feet-nine; she had alabaster skin and a head of thick, black curls bobbed short. One of my earliest memories of my mother is how I remember watching her at her dressing table. Every night she'd brush her hair one hundred times, and we'd count together. Then, she would apply her creams, always in the same order—and she taught me how to use makeup and perfume. She was very modern and had a natural sense of style. These are rosy memories for me.

I also have wonderful, vivid memories of my moments with my father. He adored me, and he doted on me when it was utterly unfashionable for fathers to behave in this manner. He'd stroke my hair and talk to me as an adult. Even though I was a mere child, he took me to the factory to show me the amazing world of spinning threads and bobbins. My father encouraged me to touch different fabrics, explaining how they were made. I was amazed at the difference between cotton and silk.

Oh, how he talked to me! I can't tell you what I ate for breakfast this morning, but I'll never forget his stories about how silk was worn by the Chinese emperor and his courtesans, how rare and exotic it was, and how the Imperial Court in the Forbidden City was closed to the world. He told me silk came from a worm. I remember pulling a face at that and he laughed. He said, "Elizabeth, there are worms and then there are worms … the silk worm is an artiste who only lives for a short time to enrich our lives."

He had a silk doll made for me that I used to take to bed with me at night.

If Mummy illustrated independence and style, Papa demonstrated a highly romanticized worldview and a talent for storytelling. He plied my imagination with untold wonders from the ancient world. I have never forgotten the story he told me about Egypt's legendary city of Alexandria.

He described the Temple of Serapis with magnificent, tall columns covered in hammered gold, lapis, and turquoise. There were precious rubies and sapphires, and sweet incense wafted through its rooms in a soft hush. Papa said Alexandria housed the greatest library the world had ever known and that artists and sculptors raced to the city hoping to work in the most beautiful pearl on the Mediterranean.

He paused in his story, and then he told me in a serious voice that Caesar set fire to the city. Everything—all knowledge and history—disappeared as though it had never really existed. This touched me profoundly. It always saddens me to think of that terrible loss, and I have often wondered—if the library hadn't been destroyed, would history have turned out the same?

Could Alexandria have been a metaphor for Papa and the world he provided me? There is an eerie similarity between them. Both were unique and remarkable; both evaporated suddenly, their beauty and grace departing with them, both changing the course of things to come forever.

Papa developed a brain tumour, and before any of us realized just how sick he was, he was gone. I must have been about six or seven. I don't quite remember, but I do know I was angry and I blamed my mother for not looking after him; I blamed her for his death. Not only had I lost my father, but in reality, it marked the end of my childhood because nothing was ever the same again.

Mummy clearly saw how devastated I was. So she told me that my father was watching me from heaven and was my special angel who might tap me on the shoulder occasionally. "When you feel his presence, say hello to him," she advised, "and tell him what you are doing. And when you say your prayers at night, talk to him and he will answer you. I want you to know that your father will always be there for you and will never, ever let you down."

I took this profound utterance very much to heart. To this day I still talk to him. I speak to him first thing in the morning and again at night. In fact, I talk to him whenever I need help—and he has always rescued me.

That I should need rescuing at all was most unfortunate, but my father's death brought a quick end to an auspicious chapter. It closed the book on wealth, security, unconditional love, and trusting innocence.

The fairytale evaporated like morning dew. A crueler reality lay in wait.

CHAPTER 2

THE DARK YEARS: FINDING THE LIGHT

What followed next was protracted misery—a pastiche of murky landscapes and unsettling interiors one finds in Victorian novels where solitary children grieve the loss of a parent or suffer alienation of their affection for one reason or another. They endure canings, beatings, ridicule, and isolation, all the while longing to redeem themselves as worthy individuals. So it was with me.

Papa was gone. Mummy did not lose herself to grief but rather insisted it was no use crying over things one could not change. She faced her situation with an incredible spirit of adventure. She was really tough, and the family nicknamed her, "The Cossack." Her philosophy was, *"Get on with it. Move forward."* I was fascinated by her strength and resolve and was certainly influenced by this. This was a mantra I adopted later on in life.

When the family lawyer announced that Papa had left a considerable fortune and a successful business intact, Mummy's response was immediate. She sold the factory and opened a restaurant. My mother, who always believed in having a grand plan, must have thought this would afford her a more independent lifestyle, but the truth is, she had no head for business and was a dreadful cook.

One of the restaurant's lunchtime regulars, a man named Isaac, soon became my mother's next suitor. Their ensuing affair was both passionate and carefree. My mother was totally in love again. She didn't care about what people said— all she cared about was Isaac. One weekend she asked her sister, Sadie, to look after the restaurant as they were going to Brighton. It was the Season. When Mummy was married to Papa they regularly spent the Season in Brighton, and she was determined to maintain her old lifestyle. Ann, who was staying overnight with the cousins, was left behind. My sister was furious—not because she wasn't old enough to take care of herself, but because she had just been left without a note or a good-bye. Ann asked Aunty Sadie for a few shillings and took the bus to Brighton. She didn't know which hotel they were staying at but remembered how Mummy and Papa always took a stroll along the boardwalk every night after dinner—and that's where she waited. When Ann saw them approaching, she walked toward them and asked why she had just been left. Mummy, arm in arm with Isaac, smiled at her and said, "It's good that you're here, you can look after your sister." And that was that. Ann stayed and Mummy continued enjoying her holiday in Brighton.

The real problem was money. My mother went through the money like a dose of salts. No one knows exactly how much she wasted, but had she been in the least bit prudent, she probably would have been set for life. Instead she stayed in Brighton for the Season and incurred a debt that, even if the restaurant was making money, she would not have been able to meet. Within three months of their return to London, Alice closed the restaurant.

The inevitable failure of the restaurant resulted in an escapade that temporarily blinded my mother's motherly obligations and they once again took off for the resort area—this time it was Westcliff, southeast of London.

Westcliff-on-sea was an idyllic vacation spot, awash in romantic cliffs overlooking the Thames Estuary and the distant Kent coastline. I think Mummy needed to get away from the criticism of the family and remarks and gossip from the neighbours. My mother's relationship with Isaac was too soon after my father's death, and many tongues were wagging. I remember Mummy telling me when I was much older how women would cross the street when they saw her coming. And while on the surface she always said that she didn't care, I know this hurt her deeply. My mother's life was always hard. At an early age she knew the only one she could depend on was herself, which is why she always played the winning hand. But since Papa's death, the cards seemed to be turning. My mother was not one to give up easily. By leaving all the negativity around her, she believed her life would turn around. *"Get on with it. Move forward."* And with that my mother decided to buy a hotel and a ladies dress shop. The hotel was a ready-to-go affair, replete with finished rooms, maids, porters, and paying guests. The dress shop was attached to the hotel, and my mother thought it would be a marvelous opportunity for Ann, who could run it. I was still very young and was left very much to my own devices.

Both Mummy and Ann worked very hard trying to make a success of this venture. I remember coming down one morning into the large commercial kitchen with its enormous table and found it covered entirely in pastries. I thought maybe it was the work of fairies. There were strawberry pastries, pastries everywhere, filled with fruits of every kind! Ann was the fairy.

She had been up all night making them. Not only did Ann bake, but she also worked in the dress shop during the day and helped coordinate the social calendar at night.

She was a fabulous salesperson and had a good eye for what worked, and the customers liked her. I think we both got our sense of style from our mother. She didn't have the largest variety of dresses, but she knew how to dress up her outfits so that they always looked different, and it didn't take long before Mummy was touted as the fashion icon of Westcliffe.

The hotel had a resident band during the season, and Ann helped round up young people and organized the dances. Yet as hard as she worked, it wasn't enough, and Mummy criticized her for everything. Over and over again I heard Mummy yell, "You're going to bankrupt me! You don't know what you're doing!" But to tell the truth, it was both Mummy and Isaac who couldn't manage. They spent too much money on irrelevant and extravagant items to fulfill an unsustainable lifestyle, and within two years they had frittered all the money away and the entire venture was doomed.

My mother pawned her jewelry. This must have been a dreadful time for her, although I don't think she viewed it this way. As I said, my mother was tough and she said, "Don't worry, we'll make a plan."

With a host of unpaid bills and debt collectors lurking at every corner, there was nothing to do but a moonlight flit. We sold off the furnishings and took off in the dead of night.

What I remember is that we used a wheelbarrow—don't ask me what Mummy put into it, because I'd be willing to bet if we'd been robbed at gunpoint, the thieves would have taken the wheelbarrow and left the contents behind. Anyhow, I remember we hopped a train and left for Manchester. Ann didn't come with us. She'd had enough of Isaac, and while she had tried to win Mummy's approval by literally giving up two years of her life, it was enough. She made contact with her father's family and went to them.

Isaac had a trade. He was a tailor—the worst tailor you can imagine! Once he made a suit for me, and I had to stand very still to get properly fitted. Well, you wouldn't have believed the mess. One of my sleeves was longer than the other, and the jacket was lopsided.

We headed north and began a long, tedious history of moving or "flitting" from one textile center to the next. We lived in Manchester, Leeds, Birmingham, Liverpool, and

Glasgow, traipsing after Isaac as he scoured the *Draper's Record*, a daily needle trade paper that fed interested parties news and job information the way *Variety* does for the entertainment industry.

He'd no sooner settle us somewhere after finding a position in a factory than he'd lose it. People eventually realized he couldn't cut a straight line—not even from a pattern.

This spotty, nomadic life was most characterized by poverty and Draconian bursts of child rearing. Mummy was expecting her third child.

Before Lynn came along, Isaac fussed over me and seemed to enjoy me. But the moment my sister was born, this ended. I became an eight-year-old pariah. Everything he had liked about me, he now hated. If I walked into a room where he was standing, he'd turn his back to me. He refused to eat at the table if I was there, so I had to finish my meal before he got home. Often he'd tell me or Mummy that my face was as ugly as a monkey's. He'd say to Mummy, "Get her out of my sight—just looking at her makes me sick." This was a traumatic, impressionable time of my life. As hard as I tried to please him, I couldn't. I never understood why he changed and spent many a night racking my brains as to what I had done to precipitate this.

I don't hate my step-father. I accepted everything that came my way. When you're a child, you tend to do that. Today, things would be different …

One day I seemed to annoy him for no apparent reason and the beatings began. My arms were covered in welts, and I constantly had a bloody nose. I didn't have a real friend because we moved so often. So with no one to talk to, I became quite reclusive and stopped eating. This was easy because we didn't have much to eat at home and as I wasn't allowed to eat at the table with Mummy, no one knew whether I finished what was on my plate or not.

Mummy served us the same thing over and over, like potatoes. They were cheap, maybe a penny a pound, and it would be potatoes for days on end. I was nervous, I was underweight, and I didn't look my age for a long time.

Mummy finally took notice of me and took me to a doctor in Manchester. He prescribed Parrish's Liquid Food, a tonic of iron phosphate compound, malt, and plenty of rashers of bacon. My mother kept a kosher home and bacon was forbidden, so she paid a neighbour to feed me. I loved eating there. I remember I would take my time, savour each mouthful, and listen to the conversation. That's when it hit me—I was no longer part of any conversation. My conversation had become a string of orders, shoutings, disparaging remarks, harsh criticisms—both at home and at school.

My neurosis also affected me at night, and I started sleepwalking, sometimes leaving the house to wander barefoot along the road until a policeman brought me home. Isaac secured the front door with a very thick industrial bolt that was difficult to open, yet I easily managed to slide it open while sleepwalking. The policeman advised Mummy never to wake me up by shaking me. Rather they had to quietly put me back to bed. This was probably one of the few times I remember Isaac being kind to me.

Clothing arrived in a hodgepodge of threadbare hand-me-downs donated by "the aunts." The clothes were hand-me-downs three times removed, so you can just imagine what they looked like by the time I got them. I would wear these awful things, which made me miserable. Mummy patched my stockings with pale pink Lyle. Pink! Apart from the hand-me-downs from my cousins (which I wore whether they fitted me or not), there was a uniform donation room at school. Girls who outgrew their uniforms would hand them in so that anyone who could not afford a new uniform could get one for free. That's where I obtained my school uniform.

I never got over those deprivations. As soon as I was able, I found a way to dress well by developing my own sense of style, just like my mother. Later on, I indulged my passion for good clothes, furs, and jewels. I guess it's one of the ways I compensated for life back then. My world as I know it now is so remote, so different, so wonderful to what I had as a child growing up, but I can tell you, I never got over that niggle of, "Oh my, look at the price—can I afford it?"

When I was eight, I noticed my reflection in the mirror. I looked dreadfully thin and white as a sheet, so I took Mummy's lipstick and dotted it on my cheeks. The teacher said I looked "healthy." This was the positive reinforcement I sought, and I continued paint my face until one day the teacher realized I was wearing makeup and hauled me into the headmaster's office. As punishment I had to stand up in front of the whole school on the stage while the nurse washed my face. This was so humiliating, and for weeks afterwards at break I was teased. I hated school and detested my teachers. My grades plunged. My savior this time was Isaac, who once again lost his job and we moved again—new home, new school, new beginning.

I was ten years old. My life had been a roller coaster of a few ups and many, many downs. Isaac's treatment of me was brutal. Daily I was told that I was not wanted, was ugly, had no manners, and would never amount to anything. The beatings and punishments were now part of my life. My life that had started out as loving was now loveless. I had no friends and no home life, and Ann, who had always been there to protect and support me, had gone.

Constantly, while walking to school alone, I'd think of things I could do to become liked. I accepted that I would never be part of the popular girls group because they were all pretty and my perception was that I was beyond ugly and hated the way I looked. I thought I was stupid because that's the way my teachers made me feel.

I remember so clearly how, while thinking about this, this became a pivotal moment in my life. There I was at such a low point thinking I have no friends, I'm ugly, and I'm stupid when—it was almost like there was a little voice in my head saying, *"Become a clown—make people laugh."* I thought if I could just do that, become a good comic, people would like me, and I made the conscious decision to be funny. This decision, all those years ago, turned my life around. I began to make friends, girls invited me to their homes, the boys let me join in the ball games, and most important at that time, Isaac sometimes laughed heartily at my funny stories.

I started to write stories and plays, which I loved to perform in front of the class. One day when I was really enjoying myself, my teacher, Miss Rollington, said, "Thank you Elizabeth, that's enough." Imagine a vaudeville act when the dreaded cane appears from behind a curtain to hook you off the stage. Well, that's what it felt like when I protested, "But I haven't finished yet"—and she said, "Oh, yes you have!" Fortunately, I didn't allow this to stop my quest, and comedy and humour became central to my life.

Our various family dwellings were a jumble of assorted rooming houses or temporary lodgings until at last we settled in Glasgow. We lived for a brief time in the Gorbels, a neighbourhood I compare to New York's Old Bowery. Characterized by mean streets, drunks, unsightly council flats, and rooming houses, it was your low down area, populated by a mix of Irish Catholics and Jews. A short while later we moved into a modest home in a better neighbourhood.

Everyone made do, especially my mother, who lived in a cloud of denial. "Poor? We're not poor. We just don't have any money ..."

Mummy still managed to hire a cleaning lady twice a week. She kept our home scrupulously clean and instilled a strong sense of personal hygiene into us.

At a time when any child only wants to fit into her surroundings, Mummy did odd things that embarrassed me. For instance, she planted glass daffodils and tulips in the front garden in the dead of winter. I'd came home from school hoping no one I knew saw me, because in my view, this was ridiculous, as flowers didn't grow in winter and I didn't want people to think that Mummy was mad.

Three years after the family had absconded from Westcliffe, the doorbell rang and there stood Ann and boy, did she have a story to tell us.

She had been kidnapped and held prisoner in Costa Rica by her uncle. What happened was that when Ann left she went to her father's family, where her uncle persuaded her to go with him to Costa Rica. He was very wealthy and promised to help arrange a very suitable marriage. Ann was about sixteen, and it seemed like her fairy godfather had arrived at last. But when she landed in Costa Rica, he took her passport, forced her to work in his warehouse without pay, and then tried to marry her off to an ugly sixty-year-old widower. By using her wits, she managed to escape while her uncle was in London on a business trip.

With Ann back, life improved a bit for me, as she wouldn't allow Isaac to hit me. But within six months, Ann married and left for London and my life returned to its normal discombobulated chaos.

With the passage of each year, life at home worsened. I was always trying to make Isaac love me, but he never did.

He cut me down at every turn, said I disgusted him, told me that no man would ever want to marry me. I was a wreck. I had no self-esteem at all. I felt ugly and worthless.

Mummy seemed to lose her feisty independence. For whatever reason, she seemed to place her faith in Isaac and became increasingly dependent on him. His words, needs, and wants became the priority. She was afraid he'd leave and turned a blind eye to what was going on. Yet for all that she *loved* him, she once said to me, "Don't tell a man everything—keep them guessing and be a bit of a mystery."

As an insight into her relationship with Isaac comes from a Manchester memory. Mummy had arthritis in her shoulder and used to go for treatments at the hospital. She had trouble pronouncing English, so she'd say she had to "fix her *soldier*" (because she couldn't pronounce shoulder). She had a special booklet that had to be stamped after each visit, and soon I heard her telling Isaac that a Dr. Miller at the hospital was in love with her and wanted her to run away with him.

Not long after that, flowers started to arrive , and the phone would ring at odd moments. Mummy always answered the phone saying, "You've got the wrong number." I remember her always smiling as she replaced the receiver

Isaac was furious and madly jealous but never confronted her about Dr. Miller. I, however, was intrigued, and when it was time to get the booklet renewed, I offered to go because I wanted to see who Dr. Miller was. When I arrived at the main desk, I asked the receptionist for Dr. Miller's office. She looked up and down the pages of the hospital directory, but there was no Dr. Miller in rheumatoid arthritis. I asked her to check the other departments, which she did, but still could not find a Dr Miller.

When I got home I told Mummy that I knew Dr. Miller didn't exist. She nodded. "Of course, I made him up. *I* sent the flowers. Just to keep Daddy on his toes ... As I've told you, it's always good to keep a man guessing ..."

The ruse worked, because Isaac believed this to the day he died. Decades later on a trip to London I visited Isaac, who was gravely ill with diabetes, in a hospital, and I told him, "Remember Dr. Miller in Manchester? There never really was a Dr. Miller. Mummy made him up."

A brief silence ensued, followed by, "Hmm." He said, "That's what *she* wants *you* to think!"

Mummy's eccentricities remain a source of fascination, and in hindsight, I find humour in some of the very things that once horrified me.

One bizarre memory is the night I awoke to see Mummy dressed like Father Christmas. What inspired her to break with tradition remains a mystery. But there she stood, tall and majestic in a red dressing gown and a fuzzy white beard fashioned from cotton wool. When she saw me she put her finger to her lips and shushed me. "I am not your mother … I am Father Christmas." Then she left a small cot made of wood with a little doll inside and some sweets for Lynn and myself.

Then there was the case of the misbegotten school Christmas cake. Cooking was one of my favourite subjects at school. We'd bring in all the ingredients and have a great time preparing fancy recipes. One year in November, a month before Christmas we made a Christmas cake (fruit cake). After it was baked, we were told to put it in a tin, seal it, and bring it back to school in three weeks to cover in marzipan. I was so excited about this project, but when I arrived home, Mummy was aghast at such a concept. "This is rubbish!" she declared. "Who eats a stale cake?" I couldn't convince her otherwise, and she refused to listen. She opened the tin and started eating. Three weeks later I was the only girl in class without a cake to ice.

The most infamous of all the humiliations Mummy ever heaped on me turned out, in hindsight, to be the funniest (but certainly wasn't funny at the time). Mummy loved going to the movies. It was the Golden Age of the 1930s when MGM ruled the world with boisterous musicals, screwball comedies, and stirring classics. New film releases were plentiful, and my mother didn't want to miss the lion's share.

Mummy really didn't speak much English and needed a translator. Every Monday and Friday I wasn't allowed to go to school. Instead she'd pack a bag of sandwiches, sweets, chocolates, nuts, and fruitcake and say, "Come, Elizabeth, it's time for the pictures."

Oh—those sandwiches! Pickled herring! I wanted to crawl under the seat, I was so embarrassed. But wait—it gets even better! I had to sit there and translate throughout the film, and all the while I could feel people glaring at us. First they'd say, "Sshshshs," and then the shush changed to "Please be quiet," followed by, *"Shut up!"* Mummy never tolerated this, and in her best English she'd turn around and say, "If you don't like it move to another seat—I paid the same like you!" Oh dear. If I could have I would have crawled under the set—anything to disappear …

In the dark, Leslie Howard and Ronald Coleman clashed with various intrigues, while Fred Astaire and Ginger Rogers sang of love. My talent for mimicry and storytelling rose to meet every challenge, and I, who was by now inured to hecklers, was ready to translate *Gone with the Wind*. I knew Mummy wanted to see the movie, so I arranged to take her. When she heard the seat was one shilling and six pence, she nearly passed out as in those days the seats were six pence. The movie was a three-hour movie. The lights went down, and the movie began

Ten minutes into the film Mummy asked me in one of her stage whispers, "Do you want a sandwich?"

I replied, "No thank you."

"Oh," she said very loudly, "all of a sudden she's become Lady Gedivy! She doesn't eat herring sandwiches."

Then later on when Vivien Leigh was digging into the earth, Mummy said again in her stage whisper that could be heard by everyone, "Why is she digging carrots? With a face like that she can get another fellow."

This continued until the interval, whereupon Mummy stood up, ready to leave. I explained that it was a three-hour movie and that this was interval. Very reluctantly, she sat, and I endured the remarks and comments until the end of *"Gone vid da Vind."*

Subsequently, years later when Ann and I were in South Africa, we spoofed this three-hour escapade on a seventy-eight record for the family's amusement. It was such a hit, it ultimately disintegrated from overuse. Everyone I knew played it—it was so funny.

I had a good friend, Leila—she had the most beautiful red hair. We used to go to dances or the movies on Friday nights and afterward returned to her house. Her mother made us cocoa and cookies. I spent almost every weekend with them, which was just fine with Mummy and Isaac. Leila's mother was so very kind to me, and to be honest, I was a little envious of the love I saw between them.

When I was quite young, I thought of myself as Joan of Arc. I knew I was destined for something great. I longed to accomplish something important for the world. But then, later on, I'd feel so defeated inside.

At thirteen, I finally discovered the meaning of self-worth. I was at an important crossroads without knowing it. The family was in dire straits and needed money, so I left school and went to work. I thought that if I could help out at home in a substantial way, maybe my step-father might love me the way he did my baby sister.

Off I went to the Labour Exchange in my school uniform, white blouse, and patched black stockings. I walked right up to the counter and impatiently tapped on it and called out, "Excuse me! May I have some service please?"

A woman with a broad grin on her face (she probably found me amusing) walked over and asked if she could help me.

I told her, like Eliza Doolittle, "I want to be a sales lady in a dress shop." She looked through a file, and spotted a job description that seemed tailor-made for my interests—a job in a retail dress shop, owned by Mr. and Mrs. Phillips. She pulled out the card and said, "Go and see these people. I think you'll be interested."

I was so excited, I literally flew to their door and arrived out of breath. They had advertised for a Girl Friday—a person with fashion flair who was honest, willing to train, clean, sweep, take inventory, unpack boxes, and unfold clothes. I was more than ready to give it my best shot.

The Phillips asked me a few routine questions, aware of my infectious zeal, my obvious youth, and possibly, my desperation, and hired me at once ... I thought they were the kindest couple one could ever hope to meet. Mrs. Phillips sat me down, offered me a cup of tea, and told me that the pay was ten shillings a week. I nodded eagerly. She then proceeded to ask me my age, and I replied truthfully that I was only thirteen.

She looked at me and said, "You're underage, so what I'm going to do for you is give you three hours for lunch."

I thought this was wonderful. She asked me about my parents, where I lived, and after what seemed like a lovely chat, she asked me if I could start on Monday. Whoopee! I was thrilled. But my good fortune was not over. As I was leaving, she called me back and said, "You know what? I'm going to give you a raise now—I'm going to give you twelve shillings and sixpence a week."

In a twinkling I received my first "wages." I was very proud of myself when I handed it over to Mummy. I loved my job. I scrubbed and dusted and cleaned—and bided my time. I was itching to get into sales because commissions paid more. I envied the saleswoman, and I watched her every move. I was always one who tried to make the best out of any situation, and part of that meant keeping my eyes and ears open.

One day, when I was sweeping out the dressing rooms, I saw a customer try on a lovely suit. She looked very good, but I knew I could make her look stunning. So I stepped over the line without permission, and blurted, "Madam, you look

wonderful and I know the perfect hat to go with that suit."
I picked the hat off the rack and handed it to her. When she
put it on and saw the magical transformation, she was amazed
and delighted and said, "I'll take the whole outfit!" I felt I had
handled my first sale remarkably well, but at the same time,
I knew Mrs. Phillips had witnessed the entire exchange from
the other side of the room and I was concerned that she might
fire me on the spot. But when the transaction was complete,
Mrs. Philips's praise was warm and effusive.

This was a watershed moment.

I had grown up in a world without compliments—
only barked orders and disparaging comments. I was truly
overwhelmed. I had just learned the value of one of my mother's
important philosophies—that you have to get on with things,
take risks, and seize opportunities. But in this transaction,
I had added something of my own. I went beyond seizing
the opportunity—I made it happen. When I realized that I
could choose to exist, or I could choose to make something
of myself, and it was a defining moment.

To make something, to become someone important,
someone who other people take notice of, didn't have to be
accomplished by telling jokes. True accomplishment comes
from the effort you put into a job to make sure that it works.
You are responsible for your own success. I had succeeded in

an area because I dared to speak up. I stopped being afraid, and I took a risk. This was truly a defining moment in my life.

I asked Mrs. Phillips if I could have a sales position, and she arranged it. Another lesson in my life—one you will hear me say over and over again—you have to ask for what you want. Nothing falls into your lap just because …

Working for the Phillips put me on the right road. I'm not going to pretend that suddenly everything was easy, because it wasn't. Nothing changed at home, but I had changed, and that was my impetus to carry on—in my mother's idiom, *"Move on, go forward, seize opportunities,"* and now armed with my own idiom—*make opportunities*—I knew I would get there.

I remained at home for a few more years, but life was still tough. I often sought refuge at Leila's house, but even there I felt very much like a child with her nose pressed against the glass, longing for—and never getting—the same familial warmth from my own family. I consoled myself with hard work and succeeded by becoming the top-ranking salesgirl at the Phillips's dress shop. I dreamed of making a better life for myself and always saved whatever portion of my commissions I was permitted to keep.

Little by little I began to object to the status quo at home even if it meant a cuff to the ears. I remember complaining to Mummy about silly things, like the way she served the soup as a last course instead of the first course. Everyone else served it as a first course, I insisted. But Mummy would stand her ground and explain that soup was meant to wash down the meal.

I began to notice everything. And the tiniest irritants made me more critical of what I felt was lacking at home. Funnily enough, I was never critical of the abuse from Isaac. I accepted this as part of normal life at home. Instead, I was critical of all the other little things.

In many ways, I was like a twisted pretzel who would spend the rest of her life untying and re-tying my many emotional knots. I was a bit of a split personality blessed with an outward charisma that radiated goodness, charm, humor, style, and a sharp mind. But inwardly, I was wary, skittish, lonely, and prone to nagging self-doubt and feelings of inadequacy.

Ann, who had already left home in a cloud of disgust, urged me to join her in London.

I was seventeen, ready to break free, ready for adventure, ready to give up trying to make Isaac love me. Oh ... I was

more than ready—I was champing at the bit to go "stompin'
at the Savoy" in search of my destiny. It was high time to
enjoy life. Being a top dress saleslady was great but not quite
enough for me. I just knew that I could do bigger and better
things with my life. I decided to travel to London and try my
luck there. Ann had a small bedsitter in London and always
promised me that when I was ready to leave home I could
come and stay with her.

When I arrived in London, Ann met me at the train
station. We flung our arms around one another; we had
so much catching up to do, and like all girls who haven't
seen one another for years, we couldn't wait. Ann described
the dance halls—I was enraptured. The fashion—I always
thought I was trendy, but the fashion in London was unlike
anything I had seen in my life! Ann told me that she had been
approached by a modeling agency to model clothing. "Next
time I go you'll come with me," Ann promised. Talk about
making a baby sister's dream come true! Modeling—this was
so glamourous ! I couldn't wait.

Ann's bed sitter was on Oxford Street—in the heart of
where everything was happening. I didn't care that it was tiny.
London was now my home. I had started my journey.

Elizabeth with Mummy

Elizabeth age 6

Elizabeth with Nanny

My only photo of my Papa with Mummy

Mummy with Isaac

CHAPTER 3

SELF-IMPROVEMENT REQUIRES CONSCIOUS EFFORT

I am at a very privileged stage in my life. I say privileged because I have lived a very long time and recognize now how important our own role is in shaping our destiny. In many ways life is like a game—play well and hard and you stand a chance at winning. Give up, play weakly, or lose focus and the chances are that you will not make it. But this doesn't mean that we always make the right decisions. Goodness me, if I had made all the right decisions I would never have done half the things I ended up doing, but this is not reality. We do what we do at the time because we believe it is the right course of action. But just because we have chosen one path does not mean that we need to entrap ourselves. To the contrary—entrapment will occur when we consciously choose not to act. We feel we are stuck, in a rut and there is nothing we can do. Over the years I have learned that we are the only ones in our lives who can make change happen. When we consciously make the decision to change, we can break the self-perpetuating circle. Self-growth requires conscious effort. In this chapter, I make reference to how I was able on many occasions to steer my life in the direction I wanted it to go and how when I put the conscious effort into making things happen, they did. And conversely, when I chose not to act, nothing changed.

When I arrived in London, Big Ben's chimes were marking history rather than time. War clouds had massed over Nazi Germany as Adolf Hitler prepared to annex Austria, and when he did, he met with little resistance. Flushed with easy success, he moved quickly in 1938 to gobble up the rest of Europe, starting with Czechoslovakia.

England stood by in those waning years, protesting, worrying, and ... waiting. Newspapers trumpeted warnings on the streets, Cockneys argued over ploughman lunches in the pubs, and women, who had lost first loves in the Great War of 1914, now despaired of history repeating. The British prime minister, Neville Chamberlain, met with Hitler, and together they signed the Munich Agreement, an odious treaty that conceded a part of Czechoslovakia to Germany. When Chamberlain stepped off the plane in England, waving the document, declaring, "Peace in our time," few believed him. It was hollow appeasement, and according to informed circles, as worthless as the piece of paper he was bandying about.

But the moodiness of the country was not about to discourage me. I had been counting the days for my joyful reunion with Ann. I was overjoyed; cramped quarters did not matter. There was so much catching up to do, so much to absorb. For one thing, London fashion was unlike anything I'd ever seen. Urban sophistication in every quarter washed over me in waves of exhilaration. Restaurants, theaters, clubs, and museums ... Speaker's Corner in Hyde Park ... the pigeons in Trafalgar Square ... Buckingham Palace and St. Paul's Cathedral—all were alive with excitement despite the gloomy news from Europe.

Ann helped me get into modeling. I remember the modeling classes as though they were yesterday. We had to learn how to walk and sit, gracefully, with a book balanced on our heads. And just when we thought we had finally accomplished this feat of elegance, along came the instructor with tea cups and saucers. She placed them on top of the books—of course there wasn't any tea in the cup. It was all about standing up straight with poise and balance.

Modeling, though, was very part time and only brought in a small income—not enough to pay rent. Even though Ann was kind and told me not to worry about anything, I knew I had to find more work. Back then it wasn't education that got you a job. It was luck and perseverance.

I walked past a local ice cream parlor with a sign in the front window that read: "Wanted—beautiful, blonde, blue-eyed girls. Must be at least five-feet-eight-inches tall. Needed to demonstrate ice creams." This kind of parlour was a new venture, based on the American novelty of girls in uniform whizzing about with soft-serve and banana splits.

Admittedly, I was slender and curvaceous, but I had *jet black* hair and *dark brown* eyes and was not what anyone would call tall. This is what held me back in modeling . Models had to be a minimum of five-foot-six, and I stood five-feet-four inches high. Having learned that one not only seizes opportunities but creates them, I entered the store without hesitation and stood in line. There was no way I was not going to get this job. I approached the manager and said, "I'm here to see you about the job."

The manager looked at me incredulously. "Now, why would I waste time interviewing you? Can't you read? Blonde, blue eyes ... tall."

"Okay, so I'm not tall and blonde, but I—"

"Look, you don't fit the description."

"You're wrong."

"I'm wrong?" He balked.

"Let me ask you … why do you want only tall blondes with blue eyes?"

"Because," he explained, as if pointing out the obvious to a child, "they will attract customers."

"Well, I understand your plan, but consider this … it'll only work for a short time because soon those blondes will all seem the same and then no one will take any notice of them. However, if you did something else, like take me, for example … well, here I am … shorter, attractive, dark haired, and a *fantastic* sales person. Picture me running in and around the taller girls taking orders. Think of it! Now, *that's* novelty. … *that's* how you'll attract attention! And I guarantee I will become the top salesgirl! "

The manager burst out laughing … and hired me.

But how on earth did I find the nerve to attempt this?

I had already learned not to accept no right away. Just because the answer is no doesn't mean that you can't do it. If you believe in something and feel that it's very important, go after it and you will be surprised how many times you find that an opening appears. But if you accept that you can't or won't be able to do what you want to, that's exactly what will happen—the door won't open and you would have lost that opportunity. Opportunities always present themselves, but if you can't see them or are fearful of opening the door, they are gone. I believe you should never give up.

Give up, slow down, don't try—none of these concepts figured into my vocabulary. Remember, I had been working steadily since the age of thirteen. I was, in modern parlance, street smart. I was used to hard work, long hours, and low wages. Like my mother, I always had a plan and moved forward. If one job didn't work out, another would. Inevitably, because of my unique drive, paths led to success. Difficulties might have slowed progress, but they never stopped me. I continued to nurse the quiet belief that I was destined to do something great; in fact, once I had taken some office job that involved being the "tea girl." I'd go around at break time, take orders for sandwiches, and then head over to the Peacock Tea Room to stand in line for takeaway with other tea girls and boys from neighbouring firms. There was this charming lad who used to chat with me—he was working at Wolfson's. He was sweet and spoke with a heavy Scottish brogue. Anyhow, he told me that he would very soon be "a somebody." I confided that I had similar plans for my life as well. So you can imagine how thrilled I was when I saw him in the film *The Great Escape*. He was Gordon Jackson. When I heard about his death a few years ago, I was terribly sad. He died too young.

I crammed my days with work; my nights and weekends, in a constant whirlwind of friends, were spent dancing and clubbing at various hot spots and hotels. Luminaries either made up the entertainment or sat at tables, smoking and drinking away the hours. Noel Coward, for one, was firmly ensconced at the very stuffy Dorchester.

This was a time when I carefully observed the manners and customs of the people I chummed with and became keenly aware I needed polish.

My friends and I used to gate crash wedding parties at the Dorchester for a lark. We'd dress up and pretend we belonged there. The ballroom was gorgeous, enormous, and lined with mirrors and sparkling studs. I struck up an immediate friendship with Coward. He could be very bitchy at times and certainly he was a legend in his own mind, but what fascinated me about him first was how he had risen to such colossal success. He came from an impoverished background—his mother ran a boarding house—yet he gave everyone the impression that his very clipped and proper speech was bred in the bone. I had heard he spoke in his enunciated way because his mother was quite deaf and this was how he managed to converse with her. Frankly, I think his English came as a result of moving in elevated circles.

At any rate, I paid close attention to him and learned a few things too.

The funny thing was, I never quite realized I sounded like a girl with a north country accent, like a character on Coronation Street, until an old friend of mine called me up one day. He had become a professor in America. Well, when I heard his voice, I squealed, "What happened to you?" because his accent was gone. So he told me he had taken elocution lessons from a woman who taught theatrical English. He gave me her number, and I went to see her right away.

I remember how I tried to sound posh when I met her, by speaking like Mrs. Slocombe from *Are You Being Served*— which was silly, I know. Without blinking, she said, "Sit down and talk to me in your normal voice." And then we began lessons in earnest, starting with vowels. She taught me not to elongate my vowels or drop my H's. I worked very hard at it. You have to apply yourself.

I am the type of person who is equally at home with farmers or royals. But when I realized how ignorant I was of fundamental things like proper speech and table etiquette, I decided to learn in a hurry so I'd never feel out of place. Don't forget, my mother was an immigrant from a small village in Russia. All I knew about setting a table was dumping cutlery in the middle and sitting down to eat. But once I got to London and lived with friends from various backgrounds, I wanted to fit in no matter what the circumstances. As I said, self-improvement comes from conscious effort. I was determined to raise the bar, and while in London I was like a sponge—observing and taking in everything.

One of my cousins, working at Elstree Studios, introduced me to makeup artistry in film.

I was fascinated by this. At last, I had found something truly creative that excited me, possibly even more than sales, and made up my mind to master this with the hope that I could turn this into a profession. At first, I trained on wooden blocks and learned all the regular tricks of the trade, and then we learned specialty makeup for motion pictures. Makeup was very different for black and white movies. An example is how we defined the mouth by using green lipstick. Red lipstick made the lips look black, whereas green lipstick enhanced the shape. I learned to make older faces look young and younger faces old. I balanced features with larger mouths or higher cheek bones, that sort of thing. And there was also hair styling, which was extremely important.

Today, when I flip through pages of *Vogue*, I smile at those tricks. It's absurd to think some readers actually believe what they see. I made up plenty of actresses with bad skin, acne, and baggy eyes. And when I was done, they looked flawless. Makeup is art. There are very few film stars who are beautiful or even who look close to the way they appear on the screen or in glossy magazines. That's where we come in. We create the perfect picture. If their eyes were small, we made them bigger. The sexy, pouting, luscious lips, we outlined and filled. If their skin was marked, we turned it into a porcelain veneer. It's the same today. I look at magazines of famous stars before their stylist makes them up and then after. It's sometimes hard to recognize them. And I am always amused when I read how a celebrity's hairstyle becomes the latest vogue and women rush to the salon for the famous cut. Don't they realize that the only reason the hairstyle works is because it is the right look for that person? It is only when you get the right hairstyle for the shape of your face and work on the perfect makeup for your skin tones that your own beauty can shine through. My advice to women—become your own stylist or if you can't go to someone and learn.

Lovely things were falling into place in London. Work at the studio kept me busy and content. I rubbed shoulders— and occasional pancake makeup—with rising stars like Vivien Leigh, Margaret Leighton, and Margaret Lockwood. It was all quite wonderful.

My early years in London had taught me to be resourceful. I had learned independence. I had learned that I don't have to accept no and how important it is to be open to change. I arrived in London without any skills and within two years had learned grace and etiquette. I learned how to walk with flair and talk with refined diction, and with my impudent humour and intelligence, I gained popularity. Those early years were good years and gave me a foundation that I could build from.

And then, the inevitable happened.

Hitler invaded Poland in September of 1939 and Britain declared war. The Netherlands, Belgium, and France fell in May 1940. What became an ignominious end to Prime Minister Neville Chamberlain led to Winston Churchill's "finest hour."

Churchill, who was not popular with many members of Parliament, faced a hostile House of Commons on May 10, and with a stentorian voice, announced: "I have nothing to offer but blood, toil, tears and sweat." With this impassioned debut, he set the tone for his countrymen. They would rally out of their fear, soldier on, and win the war at any cost by displaying the courage and discipline Churchill drew out of them. They would "… fight on the beaches, in the air, on the land, in the streets … and never surrender."

Churchill's arrival was none too soon. Later in the month, after a military disaster on the French beaches of Dunkirk, nearly four hundred thousand British and French soldiers, who had been separated from their divisions by the Germans, stood in waist-deep water, ducks in a shooting gallery, praying for rescue. British destroyers took on many of them, but the evacuation will always be remembered for the "little ships of Dunkirk," a flotilla of about seven hundred merchant marine boats, fishing boats, pleasure craft, and lifeboats. The successful rescue took approximately ten days to complete and only because of enormous civilian effort. Churchill dubbed it "the miracle of deliverance."

Next came the London Blitz, a nightly bombing frenzy that began in September and seemed to go on forever. Hitler's aim was to so thoroughly demoralize the population it would easily surrender. Oddly enough, he possessed the same blind spot as Napoleon, who had scoffed at England by calling it a "nation of shopkeepers."

Despite more than forty-three thousand deaths and one million homes damaged or destroyed in London alone, the British people dug their heels in. The bravery and resilience of the British throughout the entire war was absolutely unbelievable. The blitz gave way to regular indiscriminate bombing, day and night, willy-nilly. Sophisticated unmanned rockets fell from the skies, silent and deadly.

Over the course of five years I was bombed out three times and sought refuge with family and friends like one of the Three Little Pigs in Disney's metaphoric cartoon. At the start of the bombing campaign, I found myself running frantically one night with Ann, who was holding her baby in her arms. When we reached the closest air raid shelter located in the Underground, the street warden stopped them.

"All full up!" he said.

"Please, please … you have to let us in … we have a baby!"

"I'm sorry, ladies, but we're absolutely full. There's no room left!"

Suddenly the sky lit up in a fiery ball followed by white light and smoke. Bombs fell in quick succession, their whistling the most uniquely terrifying sounds I ever heard.

We had nowhere to run except back to the entranceway that led to our apartment house. As we stood there, two soldiers and a woman joined us. I knew everyone was feeling terrified and helpless, so I suggested we sing.

"Don't be stupid," the woman said. "If we sing we'll never hear the bombs." As she spoke an explosion ripped through a neighboring street and she became hysterical—more like unhinged.

Her screaming was so bad, Ann suddenly reached out and slapped her face very hard. "Stop it! Stop it! Get hold of yourself! You're making everyone nervous!" and as she became quieter, Ann's legs gave out from under her, and she sank to the ground. I grabbed the baby from her arms. This sort of thing happened to people all the time. I have no idea why I wasn't as scared then, but I wasn't. For some strange reason, the more the bombs exploded, the calmer I grew. My inner strength kicked in.

I don't remember exactly where I was—in London or Glasgow—when Churchill delivered his famous speech. All I remember is that I was so moved, so charged by his words, I cried and decided that I had to do my bit. An overwhelming desire to serve my country filled me.

I romanticized this decision. Perhaps Gilbert and Sullivan's *HMS Pinafore* swayed my preferences, because I fancied myself dressed smartly in nautical navy and gold braid. I was ready to take on submarines. Failing that, I'd fly for the RAF.

Well, they didn't accept me. I was so frustrated—even now, sixty years later, this still annoys me. They said I couldn't join up because my parents were not naturalized citizens, but

I wouldn't allow this to dampen my enthusiasm—I joined the land army.

While this was a far cry from the fashion and lore of His Majesty's Royal Navy and Air Force, the Land Army, the unsung hero of the war, was supported by women from every walk of life. We helped prevent national famine. We fanned out across the bucolic reaches of Great Britain, working the farms, planting, sowing, harvesting, and took up every task required in the absence of the men who had shipped out to the front.

The Land Army uniforms were not beautiful, stylish, or comfortable. They resembled earthy camouflage. They included baggy brown corduroy breeches, brogues, fawn-colored knee-high socks, dungarees, and Wellies with matching jackets and Kelly green tops. Felt porkpie hats and three-quarter length overcoats finished the outfits.

After I signed up, I was sent to Scotland to work on a farm in Ayshire. I thought I knew what I might be getting into, but really, I had no idea

To put things plainly, the "Laird" of the land, Farmer Bell, obviously believed in making hay whether the sun shone or not, and had prevailed upon Mrs. Bell to produce no fewer than thirteen children. Looking after them became part of my various duties.

There were two of us on this assignment, me and a girl named Margaret. I remember bathing the children and being sent on my first day to collect eggs from the hen house. Mrs. Bell gave me a large bucket, which I thought strange because as I poked around the coop, I only saw a few eggs. I gathered the one or two lying near each hen and ended up with a handful

"Noo, ye dinna' ken," Mrs. Bell said—and showed me how to lift the hens—no matter how much pecking rained down—and snatch the hidden eggs beneath them.

Then, we'd carefully wipe each one and pack the lot in boxes meant for shipping. I also milked the cows—there were thirty. The Bells had a bull, horses, pigs, dogs, and cats. We did whatever we had to and learned as fast as we could. I churned cream endlessly. It was exhausting, but it was also one of my happiest times.

Margaret and I wondered why we had to eat the same food every day. We ate porridge and cream, cheese and potatoes. Finally, I asked Mrs. Bell why we never found any eggs on our plates.

"We sell the eggs, m'dear—we dinna eat them, unless they are cracked or broken."

This was my cue. From that day on I always made sure to crack a few eggs, and every morning Margaret and I had eggs for breakfast. Mrs. Bell questioned this, and I made up a story about a particularly ornery hen who was the culprit. The rest of the country was rationed to one egg a week.

There was one thing I had to do that I truly hated, and that was muck out the stables and hen houses. I shoveled the lot into a wheelbarrow. Then I had to push the barrow along a plank on a twelve-inch slant and dump the contents onto a large dung hill. That took a lot of muscle and maneuvering. I didn't have muscles and wasn't very good with wheelbarrows. More often than not I topped over and the contents spilled out and I'd have to start the whole process again.

Every Wednesday Farmer Bell and his wife headed out to the village. On one occasion, Margaret and I felt uneasy about being left alone with a pregnant cow and said so. "Dinna worry, m'dears," assured Farmer Bell. "According to what the vet said, the wee one is not due for at least another week." But a few hours after they left, the cow started groaning and I called Margaret, who looked at the cow and said, "She's started.". This was so exciting. We stayed with the cow and helped deliver the calf. I remember it was enveloped in a papery caul, which we tore open. The little calf was slimy and slippery, so we rubbed him down with hay. Almost immediately he started to try to stand on his little wobbly legs, and within three minutes I remember he lowered his head and tried to butt me. This made me laugh. It was a very special moment and a memory I have never forgotten. By this time the farmer arrived and we left.

As days turned into weeks filled with green pastures and nips of cream, the dung pile grew, its flies humming a malodorous tune. One afternoon when Farmer Bell was working in the fields, I vigorously shoveled muck into my barrow, doggedly struggled up the plank, but as I tipped out the contents, I toppled over and landed squarely in the muck hill.

I can't begin to describe this to you. I had barely put pressure on one gum boot, when the muck sucked me in like tarry, gelatinous quick sand. I flailed, I screamed. No one heard me. I was sinking fast and finally ended buried up to my chin in manure. I was beyond hysterical—I thought I was literally going to drown in this muck. I am not sure what happened next, but Farmer Bell saved me. I was put to bed, and a doctor had to come and inject me because I had gone into shock. I was sent home to recuperate. When I say sent home, you have to understand that what I mean was I was told to go home—transport wasn't provided.

I packed my bag and I thumbed a lift home and rang the bell. Mummy opened the door. "Yes, " she said, "can I help you?" Mummy didn't recognize me. I had gained thirty pounds! All those eggs, that bacon and cream ...

Not long after the land army allotted me to work clean the grounds of Glasgow's Albert Park. The days were autumnal; frigid November winds whipped about, lashing faces, slipping icy fingers into the seams of outerwear. I spent hours in the weak sunshine, shivering, shoveling errant leaves into a wheelbarrow. It was the silliest thing to do. I'd no sooner get the leaves in one place then they'd take off again into the wind. I also walked about with a long iron spike with a point at the end and a bag attached to my neck by a rope so I could pick up garbage—candy and gum wrappers, that sort of thing. I collected used French letters (condoms) I spotted by the benches. It was quite disgusting, I can tell you. Finally, I reached the end of my patience with the futility of the project.

Determined as always, I packed a typical day's receipts of filthy collectibles into a wheelbarrow and marched the thing over to the curator's office. I knocked on the door, entered the office pushing my barrow, tipped it out, and angrily asked the curator , "Do you really think this is work of national importance?" He was so angry with me, but I was determined to never partake of such a useless activity again, and I told him so.

"You can send me to the navy or air force, but don't make me pick up other people's rubbish!"

His face was livid. I knew I'd crossed the line and left rather quickly. I decided I was going to leave the land army and go back to work in London, so I started to make a plan.

I returned to civilian life in London with all its pleasantries—prohibitive rationing, rooting for parsnips in Victory gardens, sitting on blankets in Anderson shelters, and stumbling in blackouts under the ceaseless threat of German bombs.

Wartime or not, the future beckoned. The only thing separating my resourceful determination from Scarlett O'Hara's was fiction. And everyone knows that truth is so much stranger.

Chapter 4

TAKE THE RISK—
MOVE FORWARD

Popular culture tends to gloss over the daily horrors of wartime London in the years between 1940 and 1945, preferring instead to emphasize the romance of the era—easy to do because tender ballads dominated the air waves and underscored the moral rightness of fighting fascism with stirring poignancy. But the reality is, for five agonizing years people rose every morning with a terrible burden on their minds. Would they live till the morrow, would their family and friends? And as they shut their gates when they left for work, they wondered if their flats would still be in one piece by tea time.

We didn't know what the future held, certainly not when the blitz was underway. What we did sense was that life prior to 1939 was gone and was never coming back, not even when the war ended. We were forever changed

It is hard to imagine living in a Kafka-esque climate approaching shell shock, where days and nights form a perpetual haze of anxiety about the next air raid siren, the next strike. Even harder to imagine was Londoners getting so used to such abnormality that it eventually became mundane.

We went to sleep night after night and heard the bombs dropping. Unless you have experienced this terror, you cannot imagine how indescribable it was. You live from day to day never knowing if you will be alive tomorrow. It's a time of extreme loss and intense fear. When the air raid sirens went off, I didn't want to get out of bed, but I knew I had to. I hated the underground shelters. The smell was putrid. I don't know if it was the smell of human fear or body odor, but it was so bad you could taste it. After a while I refused to go and instead took my chances under the staircase. And not only me—half of London was the same. Whereas at first we rushed to the underground shelters or our own self-built Anderson shelters, after a while we just stayed put inside the house and said our prayers.

As strange as it sounds, in the heart of all the chaos and terrifying bleakness, we carried on as though everything was normal. During the day we worked, and at night and on weekends, we shopped, we had tea, and we went dancing. Life was intense. We fell in and out of love, some of us married, some lived, and others died. Ann's marriage didn't work out, and she got divorced. We did all the routine things to keep ourselves sane.

At one point the city was so badly bombed, Ann and I decided to head for Scotland where Mummy was living. I remember looking out of the window of the train and seeing the whole sky lit up in an orange glow; London was on fire. The train went silent. No one knew what tomorrow would bring. Scotland seemed like our only chance; it hadn't been hit yet.

But would you believe that the weekend we arrived, the bombing started there as well? Ann and I climbed onto the roof of Mummy's apartment house and watched them fall. When the count reached fifteen, I turned to Ann and said, "You know, we may as well go back to London and risk it there." And after a short stay, that's just what we did.

In the thick of the bombing, people and businesses remained defiant. The stiff upper lip prevailed. We Brits went into survival mode. It was as if the more normal we behaved the more normal life would be.

The British spirit during war is captured in this story. Sally is weeding her garden when her husband comes rushing out of the kitchen, newspaper in hand, crying, "Sally … war is coming. I don't know what we're going to do!"

"Don't you worry, luv," she says. "Come and sit down while I make you a nice 'ot cuppa tea." Months later, while Sally digs in her victory garden, her husband rushes outside, newspaper in hand, and cries, "Oh, Sally, it's all so depressing … I don't think I can stand any more!"

"Don't you worry, luv," she says. "Come and sit down while I make you a nice 'ot cuppa tea."

Palladium Theatre had shows every night except Sunday. Artists came from all over the world to perform there. To appear at the Palladium held the same significance as a Broadway show does today. I saw Danny Kaye at least six times. Ella Fitzgerald came over, as well as the Nicholas Brothers. Even the Windmill Theatre ran nudie shows. When the blitz started, they put a sign out front that said: "We'll *Never* Close."

With blackouts in effect, strollers moved gingerly in the dark, mindful stance of the wardens of the civil defense walking their beat. Getting about was difficult during the blackout because everything was so dark. People were constantly bumping into things. We used to see a lot of black eyes in the morning. I have to tell you, you don't realize just how forceful a body in motion can be until you bang right into someone! Of course, moonlight was a big help in lighting our way, but it also meant we were sitting ducks for the bombers.

That London survived at all, with most major landmarks intact, was a miracle. It is as though the very buildings were as resolute as the city's inhabitants. At one point, when there were so many fires burning in London, the authorities didn't tell us there wasn't enough water to put them out.

The war's arrival marked an end to most commercial film making at the major studios, and once again I started job hunting. Armed with little more than chutzpah, I was able to get two jobs. I made up my salary by working at a dress shop in Petticoat Lane and Oxford Street.

Money was always tight, so I took advantage of the opportunity to let customers know I was a professional makeup artist and solicited bookings for wedding parties, photography sessions, special events … whatever they wanted. But during wartime with very little money to go around, I can't say I was busy. When you're young it's easy to juggle your time between work, fun, and sleep. It didn't matter that I worked so hard. My personality was such that wherever I was I had made sure that I would come out on top and have fun doing it.

I made the most of my situation and learned as much as I could about anything and everything. I was inquisitive about people. Call me a nosy parker, because it's what I am. One day a young woman came in to the dress shop and I could see at once she was a prostitute. I was dying to know the details of her life and work, so I struck up a conversation, and she told me she had a flat in the West End and worked outside the Regent Palace Hotel. We got on famously, and I asked her how many clients she had and you know … she seemed happy to talk about it. I was beginning to realize that people like to confide in me, maybe because I truly listen and I'm truly interested. Well, when I finished serving her she handed me a five-pound tip. Huge money! Not only that, but she did it again the next time she came in. She also brought in another "girl" who was French, very exotic looking, and wearing Je Reviens perfume by Worth. Whenever I smell it now, I think of her.

Not long after that, I was walking in the street across from the Regent Palace Hotel, arm in arm with a date, and

I spotted my prostitute friend. I waved and said hi and she ignored me. A few days later she came to explain she hadn't acknowledged me because she was working and didn't want to embarrass me. I found this sad and very touching, but I understood.

Rationing quickly became the bane of everyday existence. It was especially difficult for the British because in peace time they relied on importation of about 80 percent of their foodstuffs. With war, and the attempt of the Germans to strike supply convoys traveling to and from America, it became all but impossible to maintain normal diets. Food became so scarce that a law was passed making it illegal to waste food.

Ration coupons in ration books were as ubiquitous as fish and chips—the one mainstay that was freely available. The first foods to be restricted included bacon, butter, and sugar. Next to follow were meat, cheese, eggs, milk, canned fruit, breakfast cereals tea, jam, and biscuits. The British passion for sweets took a hit when no more than three quarters of a pound of sweets per month per person was permitted. As for exotics like bananas and oranges, they were scarce and preference was given to pregnant women.

In addition to food, clothing and petrol were also rationed. Families had a tough time stretching supplies, which gave rise to frenzied darning and home sewing, as well as inventive cooking. Apple crumble and spicy carrot cake, gastronomic staples on today's tables, originated as a result of creative wartime baking. In a show of solidarity, the chef at the Savoy Hotel created the Woolten pie, named after the head of the ministry of food. It was a vegetarian medley of potatoes, carrots, onion, and swedes (yellow turnips), done up in thickened vegetable broth and topped with oatmeal and potato crust and cheese. Authorities stressed the importance of growing one's own *Victory Garden* on whatever arable soil was available. Root vegetables of every kind were easy to raise.

Utility meals were very popular. Local churches and halls, along with Lyons Tea Rooms, offered modest three-course meals for nine pence. If you had money, you could dine more extravagantly at posh restaurants, although they were forbidden to charge more than five shillings and could not serve both fish and meat at the same sitting.

It was a very tough time, we missed so many things, I can tell you, like nylon stockings. We applied eyebrow pencil to draw seams down the back of our legs. And if you had a ladder in your stockings—Lisle, rayon, or cotton—there were stocking shops that repaired them. You could do that, or you could buy clear nail lacquer and stop runs that way.

On Friday nights we'd wash our hair with Amami shampoo. We called them *Amami nights*. Even the water was rationed. The popularity of hair washing on Friday nights entered the dating lexicon. When a girl wanted to let a guy down gently because she really didn't want to go out with him, she'd say, "Sorry. I can't make it. I'm washing my hair tonight."

I was, as always, plucky and resourceful, even in those difficult times. I'd had an entire childhood of such training. I maintained a coterie of good friends and acquaintances throughout the war, some of whom were American soldiers I'd met at popular canteens and tea dances.

If you dated Americans, you were in luck, because you could go to their PX and get all sorts of sought-after items. One time I was dating a merchant marine and he very kindly offered to bring me back whatever my heart desired from New York. He also included Mummy and Isaac in this gesture. Mummy provided a list over the phone, and then Isaac was heard to say that all he wanted was the actress Hedy Lamarr. Mummy was not pleased, I can tell you.

We all smoked in those days. Woodbines cost a penny for a pack of five cigarettes. People were always wheeling and dealing; the black market did a tremendous business. I went into a local tobacconist's one day and asked for twenty Players.

He was just about to serve me—his hands had reached under the counter—when he stopped and said, "I don't have any." So I said, "Oh no! I know you have them, I saw you reaching for them." Obviously, someone else had reserved them. Well, I got them anyhow.

If bombing, rationing, stepping over strewn rubble, death, and mayhem weren't enough to confound Londoners, a water shortage only made things even more miserable, especially when London was hit with one of the coldest winters on record. The Thames, known for never freezing over, did just that.

I wasn't as worried about a frozen river as much as I was worried about not having any hot water. I was living with my aunt near Marble Arch at that time. When the hot water went, I made a plan. I packed up clean clothes and stole over to the neighbouring Cumberland Hotel, went up to a top floor, and waited for a chamber maid to emerge from an empty room. Then I waved to her as though I were a paying guest, waltzed in, shut the door, and dove into a nice hot bath. I used whatever fancy toiletries I needed. If my aunt had known about this, she'd have killed me, but as it was, I repeated this scenario a few times and went to work happy and clean until the water returned. One winter when Ann and I were together in our flat in Knightsbridge, it was so cold, we went to bed wearing boots lined in triple thickness of woolen fleece.

We often went to the Dorchester because it was renovated just before the war. The ballroom was enormous, and the walls were lined with mirrors and sparkling studs. We all believed that it was one of the safest hotels in London because it when it was renovated the walls were reinforced concrete. There were times when the whole building vibrated and the lights dimmed, but it was true—we were safe.

I loved dancing and especially loved the jitterbug—I am a great dancer! Anyone could easily find me night after night at one of my favourite hangouts. I'd go with girlfriends, on a date, and many a time I went alone.

My favourite spot was the Astoria. On Sundays I liked to go to the Piccadilly for tea dances, which were held twice a day. They were very popular. You'd find refreshments like sandwiches, tea, coffee, cold drinks, and ice cream, but no liquor. People behaved themselves, no rowdiness. You could just dance and relax.Eventually I became a regular at the Rainbow Room, which was an upscale American canteen where they served everything American—Coca-Cola, American hot dogs, soft serve ice cream, but no liquor.

The Rainbow Room was always great fun. The music was terrific and the entertainment—the floor shows—attracted stars like Noel Coward, Danny Kaye, Edward G. Robinson, etc. They'd all come and do their bit for the war effort. Invariably, I'd meet them—if I hadn't already from my film studio work—and strike up conversations and friendships. Did you know that Eddy Robinson adored fine art? When he died, he left a huge collection of famous Impressionist paintings to a museum in Israel.

One day I met actress Kay Kendall in the restroom. This was when she was still a rising star and well before she married Rex Harrison. Anyhow, we were chatting away, and she wanted to show me a new Rimmel lipstick she'd just bought. It came with a lip brush, which we both thought was a wonderful idea. Our friendship lasted until I left England. The two of us loved joking around, and one night we decided to perform together. We stuffed our bras, blacked our teeth, and spoofed our way through "By the Light of the Silvery Moon." We brought down the house.

Kay and I got into such mischief. When Irving Berlin brought his show, *This Is the Army*, to London, we were sitting front and centre on opening night with Noel Coward, Stewart Granger, and Michael Wilding. When Irving Berlin came out to sing, he was so flat, Kay and I began to giggle. Of course, if we looked at each other, it got even worse. We stuffed handkerchiefs in our mouths and tried to control ourselves, but eventually we gave up and scurried out to the lobby as fast as we could.

Some of my warmest memories revolve around jazz pianist George Shearing, who was playing at the Rialto Club. I've been told I have a very distinctive walk and people have trouble keeping up with me. In London, my friends used to say I walked the "quick-step." Well, whenever I walked into the Rialto, George would hear me and he would stop what he was doing and start playing "Robin Hood," a little ditty dreamed up by Louis Prima and Les Brown. This became our song, and I'd always go over to him, lean on his piano, and begin humming. One of our favourite games was trying to outdo each other with poverty jokes, like, we were so poor that if anybody came to rob us, they would leave something. Well, we were so poor the church mice left us their cheese crumbs …

What a life he had! His story is inspirational because he also never let his afflictions hold him back. He was born blind, one of nine children who lived in one of the poorest parts of London. His father was a coal miner, and his mother worked as a cleaner on the trains. He was child prodigy and started playing piano at three. But because his family was so poor, he gave up his dream to go to university—even though he was awarded full scholarships—and played piano at the local pub instead. He told me, "My family needed money and I got twenty-five bob (shillings) to play." It was as simple as that.

At the end of the war, George moved to America and became a legend. Why did he succeed? Because he didn't focus on things that could go wrong. His plan was one step at a time. I remember when he told me he was going—it's always sad to say good-bye to a friend. He was so excited. America was the heart of jazz, he said, and he was going to become as great as ... as ... well, I believed him.

It took him only two years—is that incredible—two years to become a star! His record, "September in the Rain," sold over nine hundred thousand copies. That's what you call making it!

I get very passionate about stories like George's. There were so many of us who had so very little, who made a success of our lives. I look at young people nowadays who talk about their miserable childhoods and blame their upbringing for their failures and it always makes me think—what about Noel Coward, what about George ... and what about me? What about all those people who by today's definitions of tough upbringings have succeeded despite handicaps, despite all the verbal and physical abuses? We all went through tough times, and we endured what our parents put us through. We hadn't heard about rights. What matters is that you are who you choose to become. I made up my mind at an early age that I was responsible for myself and for what I aspired to be. I'm not saying it's easy. But if you stay committed and learn how to navigate through obstacles ... if you learn how to adjust, you will get there. I always say, stick with your dream, but don't be a dreamer. A dreamer is someone who never fulfills his or her ambition. A successful person works at making dreams come true

I was young, acquiring skills, reaping the benefits of an ebullient personality. It bears repeating that I was outgoing and enterprising, vastly humourous, and easy to be with. But hidden below the surface were all the hurts and lasting damage from my childhood. I never spoke about it to my peers; they saw only the confident face I wore.

One day Ann and I were walking down Oxford Street when a young man approached us and asked, "Ann, is this you?" It was Ralph, my half-brother from my father's first marriage. I had heard about him, and meeting him added a new chapter of fun and fashion to our lives in London. He was chief designer for a clothing factory and offered both of us a job. Ann grabbed the opportunity—she needed a change, but although he was loads of fun to be with, working with him proved to be a strain. He was a hard taskmaster from the old school and treated his workers poorly. He fired Ann when she had pneumonia and couldn't work for six days. I went to collect her wages. He refused to pay. I dug my heels in and would not leave until he gave me the wages, but he was stubborn, uncaring, and cruel. Eventually his partner gave me her wages from his pocket. I was furious and refused to talk to him for years.

I was staying with my good friend Val and her mother Faye toward the end of the war, and I remember watching the two of them together by the fire with such longing. How I wanted to have that kind of close family love, all those warm, demonstrative hugs and kisses from my own mother! So I decided to stop feeling like a spare part and took off for Scotland. It had been long enough since my last visit home, and because so much devastation had touched all of us, I felt certain this time I'd be welcomed with open arms. I almost didn't go because as soon as I bought the ticket I started to get pangs of anxiety and turned back to get a refund. And then a little voice in my head said, "Go home," and I returned to the train.

When I arrived home it was as if time had stood still. Mummy still complained about Isaac, and Isaac was intolerant toward me. Mummy criticized the way I dressed, what I was doing, and who I was hanging out with. This visit, however, there was one important change—me. My self-confidence had started to build, and I was determined not to feel put down. I was even more determined to spend time with Mummy and re-establish the bond we had before Isaac ensconced himself in our lives. I went with Mummy to the beauty parlour, I made tea, and I spent meaningful time with her. Of course, we resumed our custom of going to the pictures every Monday and Friday. I translated the dialogue. Our time together was time well spent, and I learned a lot about her early childhood and outlook on life. As a young girl she had no standing in the family; only boys were important. She told me stories how her father never looked at her in the eye. She wasn't allowed to talk in front of him and was made to look after her siblings at a very early age. Coming to London for her gave her a freedom that she exuberantly embraced. "I was determined that no one would ever put me down or have total power of my decisions always." This time spent with Mummy was one of the most poignant I ever had with her. For the first time I understood why she behaved the way she did. I also learned how frightened she became after she lost all the money and was now totally dependent on Isaac. I remember her sighing and saying, "Darling, I was destined for greatness, but I turned the wrong corner. I had it all and I wasted it. I was so stupid! Losing everything changed everything. Don't be like me. Don't think that just because all is good today tomorrow will be the same. You have to plan for tomorrow and save for your future. If you don't you will be forever reliant on your husband. Never lose your independence or your spirit of adventure."

Did I listen and take Mummy's advice? Of course not. In fact, I ended up making many of the same mistakes. However, I returned to London with a feeling of contentment. Forever afterward when I thought of my home life my feelings were warmed by that visit. I don't want to pretend that everything about the visit was perfect. I resented being criticized. Isaac hadn't changed. But this was the first time I felt forgiveness, and I learned that it is only by forgiving that you can move forward. This was such an important step in my life and it almost didn't happen because I so nearly cancelled my ticket. If you are reading this and are in a similar situation, take the risk and *move forward*. Forgiveness is a freedom in that it gives you the choice as to how you want to act. Riding back on the train, for the first time in my life I felt free and realized that I could do anything. My choice was now going to be about who I wanted to be. Armed with this knowledge was a power that I'm sure Mummy felt when she arrived in England all those years ago. I felt the connection.

My Papa—who I had lost at the age of six—was still very much alive in my private world. I am a very spiritual person, and I can't emphasize enough how talking with him every day helps me sort things through. He's been there for all the major problems and decisions in my life.

CHAPTER 5

LOVE BUT NO MARRIAGE

Any account of my adventures during the war would be incomplete without the mention of the three men who skirted the serious arena of matrimony.

Looking back, I can't say I was madly in love with any of them—not really. But back in those days I thought I was, and each time I fell in love it was always better than the time before. But I suppose that's the passion of youth—something I wouldn't trade for the world. Getting married before you turned twenty one was *the* thing to do then. It was a different time. If you weren't engaged at twenty-one your family started to worry. If you weren't married at twenty-four—well, it was over! Eligible young ladies were terrified of being left behind.

No one wanted to be called an old maid. That was a fate worse than death.

I ignored all that and quite frankly I forgot that I was "past it" because I was I was dating all the time. Then as now, there was no shortage of motherly advice given to women on matters of the heart. I received my fair share. Mummy had said repeatedly that a successful marriage consisted of a husband madly in love with his wife and a wife who held herself aloof. Better to be adored than the adorer. But this didn't make sense; I was young and falling in love was part of it.

Mummy went even further with me by insisting I maintain a secret fund. Having money tucked away afforded a woman independence and a means to an out, should it become necessary.

She reminded me of these things often, but on the other hand, whenever I witnessed my parents' stormy arguments—and no one tangled with Mummy and ever won—Isaac, who never laid a hand on her (imagine that!) would march out of the house and disappear for hours. And instead of feeling relieved or peaceful, Mummy would fuss and worry. She called the hospitals and the police, and she'd make herself sick until he came back.

Mummy's behavior proved that no amount of logic has ever overruled l'amour, l'amour, toujours l'amour! But this didn't stop her from imparting cautionary instructions: "A man must always behave like a gentleman," she advised. "And if anyone ever tries to make advances, remove your left shoe and give him a good hit on the head!"

Like most young people waging battles of independence, I hid much of my personal life from my parents. I dated numerous men in the 1940s; these were typically friendly, platonic relationships. I flirted with generous abandon, and though I never acted promiscuously, I was a social gadabout, flitting restlessly from one interest and person to another. Intensely curious and outwardly confident, I excelled at meeting new people both at work and socially. Most of the time I had no reason to suspect sinister motives. But one slip almost spelled disaster.

I was enjoying an evening out with a famous opera star. He was an exceedingly large man and extremely pleasant. I assumed he was as much a gentlemen as all my other friends and acquaintances, so when he invited me up to his flat, I didn't hear any alarm bells at all. I simply went out of curiosity. Well! No sooner had we arrived when he lunged at me and the struggle began. I was a tiny thing, weighing maybe a hundred and ten pounds, and he was so huge and heavy—I didn't stand a chance, and I knew it. He finally pinned me under him on the sofa, and I fought and screamed and struggled and thought I was going to die. And then, my guardian angel, Papa, stepped in. The phone rang, and he decided he had to answer it.

I took off like a bat out of hell, crying, running, and stumbling down to the street. It was very late, and a Cockney taxi driver happened by and stopped when he saw me. I was, by that time, hysterical. He helped me into the cab and I blurted out the whole ugly episode. "You're a bloody fool!" he said. "You don't go alone to men's flats!" And then he listened sympathetically and calmed me down. I was missing my handbag and jacket.

"Right," he said, "now, you wait here." And he marched up to the flat and retrieved my things. He gave me a fatherly lecture about how I should have known better and that I must promise to be more careful in future. He drove me home and was exceedingly kind. That was one lesson learned and one mistake I never repeated.

The other near-misses in my romantic adventures involved three very dissimilar men—and each one wanted to marry me.

My first serious love interest was Henry. We met at a dance before the start of the war, and we dated for a few months. When things looked like they were getting serious, he popped the question and I hurried home to show Mummy my ring. My diamond was so small—maybe less than a point. I thought it the most perfect ring any girl could ever own.

Mummy took one look at my hand and said, "Wait, let me get a magnifying glass." And then she looked at the ring and said, "You should be ashamed of yourself! You call this a ring? Better you should have made him give you a watch!"

I did feel ashamed—and totally humiliated—not because of the ring but by Mummy's outburst. Fortunately, Henry was a gentleman (or so I thought) and ignored this. Mummy then switched the conversation and started to tell him what a wonderful wife I would make. She told him I could cook, sew, iron—all these were fibs, as I couldn't do any of these things.

Then, I'll never know what possessed Henry to decree, "I think a good wife should be a fine chef in the kitchen and a whore in the bedroom." Well, that was all Mummy needed. The next thing I know my Mother stood up, grabbed him by the collar, and literally frog marched him to the front door, opened it and threw him out, yelling, "Get out of my house and never come back!" I couldn't stop laughing and eventually I posted the ring back to him and never saw him again. What a lucky escape—Mummy was definitely my hero that day.

The next suitor, one of the many Sydneys in my life, was a soldier, a captain, who had just returned from the Italian front. We met through a mutual acquaintance. He was charming, interesting, and funny. I liked that in a man. We had so much in common and fell in love. After six months, he proposed, I accepted, and Mummy and Isaac came down for our engagement celebration—I say celebration, as it wasn't really a party because of the war.

Everything was perfect except for his mother. I could tell by the way she questioned me that she didn't like me. I always felt that she thought I wasn't good enough for her son, and this annoyed me. Try as hard as I could, she had an attitude, and I couldn't penetrate the wall she placed between us. Eventually this would be one of the reasons for our breakup, but at that stage I overlooked it. Sydney was an only child, a Mummy's boy, and she fussed over him excessively.

We opened a joint savings account, I worked at my jobs, and he worked, and we'd spend all our free time together. But as our relationship progressed, we began bickering, and soon this turned into constant fighting. Our arguments often arose over a comment his mother had made, and it irritated me that he never stood up for me. His mother's criticism soon found their way into his dialect, and he started nit-picking at me. I threw the ring at him several times, which he always retrieved and gave back to me. We'd reconcile and then start fighting all over again. That ring got tossed from pillar to post, and I think it spent most of its life in his soup or his coffee cup.

I remember one time Sydney came to pick me up—I was living with Aunt Sadie—and Ann was in town visiting. He noticed she was wearing a pair of slippers he had given me and he complained about it.

"What's wrong if Ann wears my slippers?" I demanded. "I said she could borrow them ... what's the big deal?"

Well, it was a big deal to him. He was, I realized, stingy in his attitudes about me and my spending habits—and this upset me. I had worked very hard to establish my independence, and I was determined not to allow anyone to tell me what I could or couldn't do—especially as I knew I was very responsible and saved most of what I earned. We argued about the slippers and about so many other petty things it soon seemed like all we did was argue and I knew I was tiring of him and really didn't want to go through with it. I spoke to Ann, and she said this was normal pre-wedding jitters, but I recognized that we had got engaged too quickly and he wasn't the person I thought he was when we first met. He was no longer charming, interesting, or funny. I was finding out things about him on a daily basis that I didn't like and certainly couldn't see myself spending the rest f my life with him.

Then came a pivotal event. One day Sydney was very late picking me up for an engagement. I waited and worried, grew angry, worried some more, and when he finally arrived hours later, he sailed in as though nothing was out of order. I asked him why he was so late and he replied that his mother had asked him to run an errand. That was it—the final straw.

I gave him back the ring and said, "This is the last time—don't give it back to me. I don't want to marry you." He took the ring, sighed, and muttered, "Here we go again" and handed it back to me, but I shook my head and said, "No Sydney—this is it. We're done."

Of course when the family heard about this they rallied around me while all the time telling me I was making a big mistake. My mother came down from Scotland to give me a good talking to. I was getting old— this was my opportunity. How could I do this? But I was determined. I felt as though I had been released.

The last in this trio was another Sydney. He was a lot older than I was and I found him irresistible. He was charming, funny—not very handsome but just wonderfully delightful. He was a clothing wholesaler, the brother of one of my closest friends, Faye. Faye's mother adored me and thought a match between the two of us would be wonderful. The family thought it was high time he settled down.

The problem, however, was that Sydney was already involved with a married woman who lived in Scotland. The family would never have approved of her had they known she existed. Sydney couldn't bring himself to tell them about her, for many reasons, the most important being that she was still married.

I agreed to go along with him in a mock courtship, not only to help him out with family pressure, but because I really liked him and believed that eventually, I'd be the one who married him.

Sydney was loads of fun. He had a wicked sense of the absurd, a humorous mixture of wry and dry wit, plus healthy dollops of self-deprecation. He even went slapstick. One evening he came round holding sheet music and told us he'd taken up tap dancing. "No," I said. "I don't believe you."

His expression was deadpan. "Allow me to give you a demonstration." So, with a magician's flourish, he spread the music sheet on the floor in front of him and began tapping away until his trousers slid right down to his ankles. He kept right on tapping.

Another time we were at a restaurant and Sydney called over the manager to complain that I had more peas on my plate that he had on his.

I never knew what to expect from him, and that was the allure. I also enjoyed the social opportunities that came along. Sydney was well connected. Together, we attended numerous parties such as the one his sister hosted for American world light heavyweight boxing champion, Gus Lesnevich. Another memorable event was a private party for Danny Kaye.

Our pretense at courtship carried on for about a year, during which time I lived with Faye and the family. They fussed over me and made me feel like I was part of their family. They were a warm and affectionate family—and once again, privately I was seized with painful longings.

Eventually, I found this deception too much. I was in love with him, and before my heart my heart was broken, I called it off. Nevertheless, I stayed friendly with the family and Sydney until I left for South Africa.

CHAPTER 6

FROM BAD COMES GOOD

It was quiet sunny Sunday in 1945 when I was walking along a street, happily aware that the war was winding down and hoping that the end of the long, five-year siege was in sight. I was always out on Sundays, meeting friends, and on this particular day, there was an air of peacefulness marking my every step.

And then, a German V-2 rocket landed in the street parallel to where I was walking.

The ground shook, a wave of debris hurtled through the air, window panes exploded, and the last thing I remembered as the force knocked me down was turning my head away.

What ensued was chaos—cries and groans rising from thick smoke and plaster dust, buildings and asphalt torn asunder, limbs and bodies, alive and struggling, or gangling and quiet.

I don't recall events in any straightforward way, it's been so many years, but I do remember how everything seemed to happen in very slow motion. Sight, smell, taste, touch, and sound shift from real to dreamlike. Sounds became muted—it seemed like people were slowly floating past me with outstretched arms and open mouths. I couldn't hear what they were yelling because amidst the chaos was an enveloping silence. One minute life was normal. Mothers were pushing their perambulators (that's an old fashioned word for pram). A man was hailing taxi. I smiled as I passed a couple. He was tenderly stroking her tears away—it was clear he was soon leaving for the front. Two women were gossiping over their fences. One had a blue scarf tied around her head with curlers peeping out and the other was wearing a dirty apron. .I critically glanced at them and thought, *For sure that's not going to be me in ten years time.* I remember that it was a clear day for a change—the sky was blue, the sun was shining. The street wasn't that busy. This is why I was walking on Hanson. It was my walking route to Oxford street. Had I taken the bus I would not have been there. Had I not been rushing, I would have missed it. Had I only made one small change my life would never have turned out the way it did.

As I said, one minute everything was normal and then the next second utter madness and confusion. I ended up in a sitting position, staring. I had worn a lovely coat that morning—black, with a sewn-in A-line bolero and three enormous gold Galleon buttons, and it was ruined. How silly, when you think about it. There I was, my face was dripping, I was covered in blood, and I was upset that my coat was ruined!

Medics took me by ambulance to a nearby hospital. I knew something dreadful had happened to my face, and while this may seem trivial now in the scope of the tragedies that befell the rest of the people, I was terribly afraid. The young doctor attending me was about to place a sheet, probably gauze, over my face to clean the wound. "Stop!" I screamed. He didn't understand and picked up the cloth again. I was so afraid this would rip my skin even more that I pushed his hand away and started crying . "I don't want to be scarred." The doctor, who probably looked at me and thought, *It's too late for that as you are already scarred*, pretended that all was good and despite the fact that the emergency room was packed with war victims, he sat there with his tweezers and picked out all the debris and glass splinters he could find. He was very patient and kind, and when he finished he held my hand and said, "You are one lucky girl. The glass missed your eye by half an inch. You're going to be fine." I tried to smile, but my mouth but I didn't work. I heard this all in muffled tones, for while my vision was spared, my hearing was not. I paid little attention to the good news. Instead, I focused on something else the doctor was saying. "I'll be honest with you, Miss. I've done the best I can, but you should know you are there will be permanent scarring ..."

I went to Aunt Sadie's house, who said she would look after me. Aunt Sadie was a small woman with the same curly black hair as my mother. She had a small tip-tilted nose and was the sweetest person I've ever met. Nothing was too troublesome. She was loving, kind, and gentle and helped care for me. For weeks I stayed hidden from view. It was no good looking in the mirror, no good at all, because the redness and swelling were slow to subside, and the various pock marks and craters left by deeply embedded glass mocked me.

My private world turned as surreal as Hyde Park, which I used to pass every day. All the fencing around the park had been removed for the war effort. In fact, all the railings (fences) in London were appropriated to melt down for armaments. Even our railings were taken. At the end of the war we found out that most of them were not used and were thrown away— what a waste! The removal of the railings around Hyde Park opened up the park and gave us easier access. For the first time in the history of the park anyone could walk through the park any time of day or night. But, and this still makes me laugh, the gates remained standing as straight as a sentry. Every night they were securely locked as proper civil etiquette demanded. This was so illogical and in my opinion typifies the absurdity of English protocol. Every night an officer trekked up to the gates, closed them, and took out a very large key and locked them. Why?

The absurdity of that lone gate protecting nothing unnerved me. Now I thought, *How cruel and indifferent the world is!* I had, thus far, literally spent my childhood and youth trying to survive, to get ahead, to keep myself optimistic despite financial and emotional deprivation and extreme feelings of alienation. And now, just when things looked like they might be improving, a joke of the meanest kind had consigned my appearance to the trash bin. How was I to work as a sales woman, a model, or a film makeup artist, working on some of the world's most beautiful faces with a face that might provoke instant revulsion?

My entire personality changed. I became quiet. I was depressed. I was baffled by the unfairness of everything. I was living in a bleak stupor. My usual optimism turned to dark pessimism. I needed to heal, I needed to work to earn a living, but I didn't know how I was going to face the world. In a nutshell, I felt very sorry for myself and didn't want to live.

I took to wearing hats, large sunglasses, and grew my hair longer so I could comb it over my face and neck. I used Leichner's Professional Kamera Klear pancake—a heavy stage makeup I used to when making up the stars. It helped to hide the blotches and pocked complexion. But this was only makeup, as I was reminded every day when I washed the makeup off my face and there staring back at me was a face I didn't know.

I have always believed that life is a series of lessons open for each of us to learn and grow. Looking back, I know that I ignored many of the lessons offered and only realize now how much time I wasted by not heeding them. Lessons come by way of events, a little voice in your head, someone says something to you, something good happens, something bad happens—lessons are always there.

When my skin was damaged, I became so self-centered and was all consumed by bitterness and self-pity. I didn't want to live. I refused to see my friends. I spent a lot of time crying. Never once did I ever say of prayer of gratitude for the fact that I survived a devastating explosion. I survived when others around me didn't. I was so self-absorbed I didn't care about anyone else. I remember when my Aunt Sadie told me about a friend of hers who lost both parents in that explosion and

I'm ashamed to admit that I turned to her and retorted, "I'm sorry to hear about that, but I'm also suffering!"

During this time I lost all sense of creativity and fun. I stopped dancing and refused to listen to the radio. My family desperately tried to get me to go out. I suppose they had enough of me as well—no one likes a misery—but quite frankly I didn't care about them it was all about me. Eventually I had to go back to work, but my performance there was very mediocre, and on more than one occasion I was called to order. Finally Ann couldn't take it any longer. "Enough is enough," she said, storming into my room. "Get dressed. We're going out." I grumpily followed her and some semblance of normality began, but then it crashed again.

One Sunday, I had a date with a man named Charles and arranged to meet him at Marble Arch. I waited and waited but he never showed up. We were supposed to go dancing. After thirty minutes I went home totally depressed. In my head I was convinced that he didn't show because I was so ugly and my world turned dark again.

A few weeks later I spotted him while I was walking down Regent Street. He was walking toward me and I instinctively started to cross the street so I could avoid him, but before reaching the other side, I stopped and turned back.

Just seeing him made me so angry, and this anger infused an energy into me that I hadn't felt in months. I marched straight up to him and angrily asked why he hadn't bothered showing up. He looked at me with tears in his eyes and in a flat voice told me that on Sunday, a V-2 rocket made a direct hit on his building and that he lost his mother, father, and two sisters at eleven in the morning while he was out buying the newspaper. He put his head on my shoulder and sobbed.

This was my turning point. I put my arms around him. I made up my mind there and then that I was going to survive this war and to do this I needed to rebuild my inner strength.

I am going to make it!

Six simple words changed my life. Now that I knew I would make it, I started to make plans. I wrote this in the front of my diary:

1. As I get up every day I will say to myself, "Today I will make it."
2. My face is not my future—I am responsible for my success
3. I choose to be strong
4. I choose to go forward

5. I will always be there for those who need me

These five principles became my foundation, and later I had this made into a plaque that is still displayed on my desk.

Charles and I developed a solid friendship. While helping Charles cope, I learned how to live again. Charles was a scientist but not a boffin. Quite the contrary—he was fun, on the ball and not at all boring. We went dancing, watched the movies, and sometimes even dined out together.

It was during this time that I started to work with other war victims. I visited hospitals and spent time reading to patients. With every person I spent time with I made it my business to find out at least one important fact about them— who they loved, where they lived, what they did before the war. I have learned that there is always something special about most people in this world. When you take your time to find out what this special quality is, that's when you have a relationship.

My objective with each visit was to make sure that the saddest person I met smiled.

We seldom realize the effect we have on other people. How often do you walk past someone and inadvertently glared at them? Or better still, how often do you look right through someone because your thoughts are far away? This can be devastating on the recipient.

I remember another time, before I was wounded and was living in Gloucester Terrace. Every day I used to pass a small, crippled man sitting on an orange crate outside the tube station on my way to work. He sold newspapers. I bought the *Daily Mirror* for a penny every morning. And every morning I'd always say, "How are you? Have a lovely day, my darling!"

Well, one morning I was in a mood. I don't remember what I was so upset about, and I ignored him completely. The next day, when I asked him how he was, he said, "I think yesterday was the most miserable day of my life. You know, you are the only one I look forward to seeing, you're always my ray of sunshine and yesterday you cut me dead. I didn't know what I had done …"A kind word means a lot to people. Take your time to make time for those around you. Ultimately you are the one who will benefit, because life is a circle.

I befriended the doctor who had treated me in the emergency room and often used to pop in for a quick visit, a fun chat, a spot of levity, and a smoke. Yes, believe it or not, in those days, doctors used to smoke in their rooms while examining patients. During one particular visit he had to excuse himself from the room to answer a telephone emergency.

This is where serendipity stepped in. This is how I came to realize that nothing happens without a reason, even if we do not know what the reason is at the time.

Thumbing idly through medical journals, I waited for his return. As I skimmed various pages, I discovered an article detailing the use of a new compound that was used to treat wounds on the war front. I didn't hesitate. I pulled a pen and paper from my handbag, furiously scribbled down the salient details, and then tucked the paper out of view. Sure enough, when the doctor returned and saw me pouring over stark medical photos, he chided me and whisked the journals away. I asked him about the new treatment and he benignly said, "Elizabeth you wouldn't understand—this is a medical journal for doctors." We resumed our conversation, but throughout, I sensed a vibration pulsing in my purse. It was all I could do to remain still.

As soon as I was able, I hurried to see Charles.

"Charles, what's this? Do you know anything about it?" I handed him my notes.

In a second or two he said, "Yes, I'm familiar with it. Seems quite promising."

"Can you make me some? Or write a script?"

"Make you some? Don't be silly. It's still in experimental stage. It's not for the public. They're trying it out on the war wounded."

"Charles, what do you call me, then? I am one of the war wounded!"

He finally agreed, and I soon came into possession of a serum containing a compound of marine ingredients that would eventually be known as Torricelumn™. By today's standards, it was a crude version—all the more remarkable because it behaved like a miracle in a bottle even then.

I am pretty sure I was the very first person ever to have a beauty treatment in a serum. Charles said serum penetrated faster into the skin. I used it every day without fail. Charles kept supplying me, and gradually over time, my face healed completely. Not only did the Torricelumn™ speed the healing, but it also boosted the luminosity of my complexion. My skin, which had always been one of my most attractive features, looked remarkably radiant. Matching this new radiance was a brightness that returned to my perspective. The tarnished penny had made way for a newly minted version.

I was now in possession of a product that would change my life completely and didn't quite realize it. Torricelumn™ and I were destined to become as uniquely famous and inseparable as Coco Chanel and her No. 5, for you simply cannot speak of one without the other.

As the months of my healing sped by, I noticed people were mumbling. Annoyed and frustrated, I said to Charles, "You don't speak clearly." Charles suggested the problem was mine.

I really hadn't noticed I that my hearing had deteriorated after the bomb blast, but I refused to take any notice and carried on regardless. Much later after I was married, Ann suggested I have my hearing tested. True to my mischievous, quick-silver humour, when I did eventually go for the test, I was asked to repeat whatever word I heard in the headphones. The first word was "apples" and I said "assholes." Severe hearing loss in my left ear necessitated a hearing aid. I balked, I despaired, I staunchly refused to wear one—and I finally went for it. My mother had always said, "What cannot be altered must be endured."

The war ended. Life, as I knew it, was slowly returning to normal in the sense that I was working hard, putting up with hard times, and looking on the bright side. Work at the film studios picked up, and I took on more assignments. One day, an actress with dark hair and striking looks struck up a conversation. "You have such a beautiful skin," she observed.

"I just hate mine lately. Too much makeup, the lights are killing me …"

I beamed. Beautiful skin was something I never thought I would hear again, and I told her my story.

"I can't believe this. Your story is remarkable—do you have any for me?" she asked. I scraped around in my handbag and found a small bottle of serum. " You can have this. I'll get some more."

The actress accepted the serum and that was that—until sometime later when our paths crossed again. She was in the makeup room. I had to look twice as her skin was transformed to a beautiful, fresh-looking, glowing skin. This was the first time I had seen what it could do for other people. Objectively, I appraised the true impact of the serum, and it was remarkable. She was just as enthusiastic. "I just love what it did for me, Elizabeth! Tell me, where can I buy this?"

A lightning bolt moment!

It truly had not occurred to me that I had a product to sell. I hadn't considered it at all. But the moment the subject came up—this was my "a-ha moment"! And I knew in that instant what I was going to do, perhaps what I had been destined to do.

I am known for my power of positive thinking, for my many useful mantras, one of which is "from bad comes good"—an inspiration I press on any person in despair.It was like a jigsaw puzzle fitting into place, helped along by luck, faith, and the constant presence of my guardian angel, Papa. If I hadn't been out on that Sunday afternoon, I would not have been hit by bomb blast. If my face hadn't been damaged, I might not have visited the doctor when I did. And if he hadn't had to leave the room, I might never have read about Torricelumn™—and who knows how long that medical journal was lying about?

I truly believe this was God's gift to me. I was going to help women everywhere. I was going to make women beautiful. This would not happen overnight, but now I knew where my destiny lay. I had spent my young life preparing for this role. I was eternally caring and curious, always wanting to help and assist—one of the reasons I was so effective as a salesperson. I had enormous reserves of strength. I was passionate, well spoken, uniquely stylish, bold, and determined—and I owned a wry and bubbly sense of humor. The word no was not in my vocabulary, just like Mummy.

As for Charles ... He was the sweetest, the most kind, gentle man, a sweet and good soul. Charles found happiness again. He married a nurse. We remained friends until his early death. I had been in South Africa for about ten years when a letter arrived, addressed to me from Charles's widow. "I want you to know that Charles always told me how you saved him and that he owed his life to you," the words said. The letter was so full of warmth and appreciation, so tender in its regard for the relationship between us. I had to put the letter down and I cried. In so many ways, I owe my life to Charles. He was my turning point. It was because of him that I chose to live and become who I am today. Thank you, Papa.

CHAPTER 7

THE PAST HAS TO BE MANAGED, NOT IGNORED

One would assume that with the war over and the last of the troops home, London sprang to life in glorious jubilation. But celebrations were short lived. Post-war rationing was worse than ever, and not all the men returning from the front found jobs waiting for them. Buildings lay in ruin, the economy was depressed, and supplies of every kind were hard—if not impossible—to obtain.

It was really tough because we all believed that our lives would improve after the war and they didn't. Ann was fed up and made plans to immigrate to South Africa. She had still not gotten over her divorce. I know she was still in love with her ex-husband despite the fact that he had hurt her to the core. Ann sent letters constantly begging me to join her. She talked about the wonderful sunshine. She raved about the fresh fruit, eggs, and meat—all sorts of food we hadn't seen in London in years. And she kept reminding me about the availability of nylon stockings and fashions. The stores were fully stocked and carried everything one's heart desired. Her letters arrived twice a week, positively delirious with praise

I pondered these revelations in depth. We had shared flats together in town, and were, since childhood, used to a nomadic life. Even now, after my year-long, heart-breaking pseudo-engagement to Sydney was over, I had moved from Faye's home to my Aunt Sadie's in Gloucester Terrace. But a move all the way to South Africa? I was lonely and still missed Sydney, and the more I thought about it the sunnier South Africa became. I'd need to save oodles for the steamship ticket, and in the final analysis, it was a daunting and permanent-sounding prospect. In the interim, as Ann's letters accumulated with repetitive effusive refrains, I soldiered on, working and saving through record cold winters and a sputtering economy.

Intrepid and enterprising as always, I continued to juggle as many jobs as I could handle. There were studio assignments and in-house modeling stints in the fashion sector. I worked at a furrier and I even dabbled for a time as a waitress at a vegetarian restaurant near the dress shop I also worked at on Oxford Street.

In addition to this running around, I was also selling my private collection of Torricelumn™ serum to anyone and everyone I met. I was probably making everyone sick with my obsession, but I was absolutely driven to make this a success. I wanted to set up a mail-order business, although any kind of serious mass manufacturing was out of the question. Undeterred, I sold door to door, at makeup parties, and to clients I had already established. I seized every conceivable opportunity and was never without product in my handbag. My serums cost roughly five shillings and sixpence, which was more than reasonable.

Working at the furrier was very slow because of the sales hierarchical system. It was a ridiculous setup, really. They had a pecking order for the sales staff. If a customer walked in, sales woman number one handled the transaction. If she finished that sale and yet another customer entered the shop, it was her client—and commission—once again. When more than one person walked in, that's when the rest of us could spring into action. I was sales girl number three—and you can imagine how impossible that was at a time when furs were so highly taxed. And in the summer? Forget it! This was still post war, and most people couldn't indulge in luxuries like that. It was a tough sell, a challenge.

When we had slow days I'd duck around the corner to Willerby's for the afternoon tea dances and I'd leave instructions with one of the other sales staff to call me if the shop was getting busy. Off I'd go for a cup of coffee and I always had stock in my handbag ... just in case.

On one particular afternoon, a stranger made quite an impression on me. I was sitting by myself looking around at the many couples huddled at little tables, and I spotted her, also on her own. Well, you *know* I'm a nosy parker, so I looked her up and down, noticed she was middle aged and well groomed, and I walked on over to her and said "I'm alone and you're alone, may I join you?"

The woman thanked me for coming by and said she often dropped in because she enjoyed the music and the general company. We struck up a conversation, which was as an eye-opening learning opportunity. The whole time she talked, I sat there with my chin cupped in my hands, listening to her every word.It was a sad story, really. "I had a very good life," the woman explained. "I was very happily married, with grandchildren, and a husband who made a wonderful living in the garment industry. We had a beautiful home in Golders Green. No complaints at all. Well, one afternoon, my sister,

Frieda, called me and said she had seen my Harry walking on Regent Street with a very attractive blonde. So I told her it was probably just one of the models working in his showrooms. And when Harry came home at six, just as he always did, I casually mentioned Frieda's call. Harry said it couldn't have been him, that it just so happened he'd never left the factory all day.

"So I told Frieda this, and she was quite insistent. 'It was Harry. How long have I known him? Of course it was Harry!'"

The inevitable confrontation followed, until the truth tumbled out. Harry had been keeping a mistress in a flat for twelve years. He broke down. He was a mess of contrition. But his wife couldn't say a word. "My face froze," she me. "I literally could not move my mouth."

Harry went on. "I swear to God, I have been trying to get rid of her for a long time. It's finished now, you hear me? Over. The woman's been driving me crazy anyhow."

Now her tears flowed ceaselessly and Harry, clearly agitated, said, "We'll fix this—I'll fix this! We're grandparents! I love you. I'll do anything to fix this! We'll sell the business, sell the house. We'll move to Brighton and start fresh!" He cried, he begged, he pleaded.

I sipped my coffee and asked, "Then what? Did you go?"

"Yes—and that's when I made a great mistake. I couldn't trust him anymore. We moved to Brighton and tried to get on with our lives, but I wouldn't let it happen. I nagged him morning and night. Every time he went out I nudged him, said something tart or sarcastic. I couldn't control myself. And then one morning he went out for the newspaper and I never saw him again. He just walked out and never came back.

"I ended up packing up the house and moving back to London on my own. So here I am now, alone and lonely."

I offered comfort to my tea-dance acquaintance and encouraged her to look at her situation like the end of a chapter, not the end of her life. I assured her that she was still an attractive woman with a future. I told her my story and how out of bad comes good—that's where you have to go—move forward. Make a new life for yourself. I cheered her with amusing stories and soon had the woman laughing.I really learned from that unfortunate story how important it is to turn the page and move on. Forgiveness is about letting go.

I decided to follow Ann to South Africa. I had saved my money and managed to raise forty pounds in a matter of months, so that when I presented myself at the Cunard ticket offices, I was already champing at the bit.

"I'm sorry, Miss, but there's a wait list. It could take months."

I pleaded with him, to no avail. I finally rose from my chair, thanked Mr. Hamilton, breezed out of the office, and called him an hour later. "Mr. Hamilton, it's me, the one who was in a short time ago. Has anything changed? Any new cancellations?"

The answer was no. But no never stays no for long when I am determined.

I kept calling him, I nagged him daily, until finally he refused to take my calls altogether. So then I used a disguised voice, and I even got friends to call up and as soon as he came on the line, he found me waiting and asking. My campaign looked like it was doomed, but apparently, Mr. Hamilton had reached a breaking point. "Can you be ready in three days?" he asked.

"Mr. Hamilton, I am ready now! I'm packed, I have all my papers. Yes, I am ready!"

"Very good," Mr. Hamilton said. "I am going to get you out of this country if it's the last thing I do."

Happier words were never spoken. The fog had lifted. I left the country in the late 1940s, spurred on by London's melancholic zeitgeist and the ridiculous paucity of food and everyday staples. In those waning post-war months leading up to my departure, I stood on shifting sand. Everyone was getting on with the next chapter in their lives, or moving away. George Shearing left for America, Kay Kendall landed her first major screen role in *London Town*, and my sister Ann was waiting to welcome me in South Africa.

CHAPTER 8

LOVE IS BLIND—A TRUE RELATIONSHIP IS ABOUT TRUST AND HONESTY

Aunt Sadie came to see me off at Southampton. The night before she had thrown a Bon Voyage party for me in London, which was both happy and tearful. I was bubbling with excitement—eagerly anticipating what life would be like in South Africa. People asked if I was nervous about sailing off that way, all alone. Not at all. It was an adventure. I was so pumped and ready to go. I believed my future awaited me in South Africa—a future that included love, marriage, success, and happiness. I asked Aunt Sadie to write that on the cake that was brought in at midnight adorned with lit candles to celebrate all forthcoming birthdays. I started to cry when they sang, "Happy Many More Birthdays" and really cried when we all linked arms and sang, "Auld Lang Syne." Even today, every New Years Eve tears well up when we sing the song. It's a wonderful memory.

I checked into my cabin, which I shared with two kind missionaries—nuns, actually. One kept her teeth in a glass. They were very kind and mothered me. Luckily, I never got sea sick, and life on ship was grand. It was like being on holiday. Every night I went dancing, and during the day I'd get up late, go for lunch, and have tea with the girls. In fact, when I thought about it, this was the first time since I was thirteen that I hadn't worked, and I was having a ball!

Every day at 3:00 pm the purser rang his bell and walked around with a notice board of names. If your name was on the board, it meant that there was a telegram for you. I never expected anything and usually didn't even look in his direction. One day I did look at the board and my name was there. I remember being so excited—to think I had a telegram! While walking to the desk I imagined who it could be:

Sydney 1—no, that was final

Sydney 2—hopefully not

Mummy—I hoped all was well

I clocked off everyone and when I reached the telegram desk I have to tell you I hesitated before walking over as by now I'd become a little apprehensive. *Ha! Ha!* It was the girls from the dress store wishing me luck. It was a thrill, really. Quite unexpected. I smiled all day.

As the days stretched before me, I held fast to my sense of wonder, my secret hopes and dreams. I was in my twenties, and an entire world of possibilities lay waiting. I wondered whether I would be able to sell my serum as successfully in South Africa as I had in London. Ann was modeling and already promised me that she would help me get a job. I really felt confident. It was such a change from when I was a young, gawky schoolgirl.

We had a brief stopover in Madeira. I bought myself a straw hat and a bunch of bananas. We hadn't seen bananas since before the war. And when I offered some to the stewardess on board, she looked at me very curiously. "You remind me of someone," she said. "I can't think who—wait! Must have been almost a year ago ... another girl did exactly what you did. She bought a straw hat and bananas as soon as we stopped here ..." After a bit of probing, I realized the other girl was Ann. Same ship, same stewardess. This sort of coincidence always sparks a kind of mystical association with me when I consider my life.

Cape Town came into view about ten days after I set sail. The ship docked at 6:00 am. I had woken early as the captain announced that the sailing into Cape Town was like going to the eighth wonder of the world. Luckily it was a clear day, and the view of the mountain against a tanzanite blue sky is a memory I will never forget. Cape Town was like entering a sun-filled paradise!

I eagerly made my way down the gangplank with a throng of excited people, many of them, like me, en route to the city of Johannesburg. While on ship I learned that the fastest and most luxurious way to Johannesburg was on the Blue Train, but as we arrived a cry rose from someone: "We've missed the Blue Train!"

I hurried to the first travel agent I could find to ask when the next train was going to Johannesburg. It wasn't for a few days, and then he asked me if I wanted to fly. I purchased a ticket without a second thought and sent Ann a telegram explaining I'd be flying in the next day. I checked into a hotel and decided to do a bit of exploring and took a bus to a place called Sea Point. Of course, I hadn't a clue how far away that was, so I made sure the driver let me know when to get off. Well, soon I saw hotels bordering the sea and knew I was in a resort area, and when I stepped off the bus, I looked around for somewhere to put myself and spotted a bus shelter. I sat on a bench, stared out to sea, and noticed my ship in the distance.

An elderly, gray-haired woman was knitting in the corner of the bus shelter. I pointed to the ship and told her I had just come off that ship. The minute she spoke, I recognized a Yiddish accent. It was so familiar and welcoming in such a far-away part of the world. "Come with me, we'll have lunch," she said. And just like that she took me to her home and made us lunch. It was marvelous. We talked and ate, and I remember how she took out her photo albums and showed me her family. It was such a homey experience and gave me a feeling of comfort. After that it was time for me to go, and she insisted on walking me back to the bus stop, giving me all the directions I might need. We said good-bye she kissed me, hugged me, and wished me, "Luck! Luck! Luck!" I don't remember her name, but I'll never forget my first welcome to South Africa.

The next day I arrived at the airport. You have to understand I'd never been on a plane before—very few people flew in those days. First experiences are always the most joyous. The first time we ate ice cream, kissed a boy, wore high heels—I'll bet that you can remember all these moments. So it was when I stepped into that plane. It was noisy and very uncomfortable, but that didn't deter my overwhelming enthusiasm and exhilaration. Immediately I started to write a letter to Mummy, Aunt Sadie, and my friends back home.

The plane touched down at Jan Smuts Airport on the outskirts of Johannesburg. The air was very dry and dusty. I had to close my eyes against the glare of the hot sun and then I heard, "Liz! Liz! There, waving wildly, was Ann. We hugged tightly, and Ann didn't stop talking. Amazed that I had the nerve to fly on a plane, she wanted to know *everything!* And then suddenly she stopped blabbering, looked at me, and said: "Goodness gracious! You've had a poodle cut! You look so cute."I had always worn my hair, which was jet black, shoulder length but figured I would do something different for South Africa. I loved the "chicness" of this new style. I felt like a change, an updated look for a new life.

The trip to Johannesburg from the airport seemed to take forever . In London everything was always around the corner, in walking distance or a short bus ride away. At least that's what it was like for me. Going from the airport to Johannesburg was like going to a distant place—or so it seemed. I looked out the window and saw miles and miles of grassland. The window was open, and I remember feeling quite short of breath. Ann explained that Johannesburg was six thousand feet above sea level—it was like living in the mountains—but we weren't in the mountains just high up.

"You'll get used to it," she said. This made no sense. Ann told me that water took less time to boil things. Soft-boiled eggs only took three minutes, not five minutes. There wasn't a subway, and the busses were unreliable. I began to think that I really had come to the opposite side of the world. Ann's apartment was huge. She had described her apartment in her letter when she asked me to come to South Africa, but I thought she was exaggerating. It had high ceilings, each room looked like a living room, and best of all was the outside patio. In London we had an adequate flat—but this seemed like the height of luxury. I started to feel comfortable and at home very quickly.

That night we went out for dinner and for the first time since the land army I had steak and "real eggs." I must have sounded like a simpleton because when the waiter told us that steak and eggs was on the menu I said, "Real eggs?" He looked at me peculiarly, and Ann laughingly told him I was just off the boat. After all these years I can still taste that meal.

Ann helped me get a job at a dress shop as an in-house model and commissioned sales assistant. I loved earning commission, and within a short period of time I was earning a lot of money. Soon after arriving I moved into my own flat and started researching who could make up my serum, but this was harder than I imagined it to be. Life seemed easier in Johannesburg, yet I missed London terribly, and every week I wrote home. I had promised to write to everyone, and I kept this up as long as I lived there.

Socially I hadn't met anyone I really liked. One night I agreed to go on a blind date with a fellow named Cyril, who was a bit of a bore and not well dressed. I thought this of most of the men there compared to the English gentleman I used to date. It wasn't at all what I was used to, and I never grew to like it either. London men were so much more fashion conscious. We went to the Sheraton Hotel and caught the floor show.

I noticed the saxophone player right away. He was well dressed and had a wave in his hair. I leaned over to Cyril and said, "That guy's from England." Cyril said he wasn't and furthermore he was married to the singer in the band. I insisted he was wrong about the English bit.

Well, when the music stopped, the sax player, Sydney—yes, another Sydney—came out front to do a floor show, a magic routine, for the audience. He was carrying an easel. He asked people to suggest numbers and ended up drawing two figure eights and a one on the easel. I watched him turn these three numbers into a face. It was amazing. He was so artistic—you could see that immediately. He was terribly quick and clever, and his speech was musical and cultivated. I knew he was a

Londoner, and I knew I wanted to meet him. I couldn't take my eyes off him and completely ignored poor Cyril

When he finished performing, he came over to our table and asked if he could join us, and at that moment, I knew I was in love. He was perfect—tall, dark, handsome. His voice was melodic—I was under his spell. During the conversation I learned he was not married to the singer in the band and was, indeed, a Londoner. I probably gave Cyril a smug look at that. I told him I was from London too. "Why don't you ask Sydney to come to your party next Sunday?" I innocently asked Cyril. To my delight, he did, and then, looking at me, he asked Sydney to bring some girls along.

I had to work the next day, Monday, and when I walked in I told my friend Judy that I had met the man I was going to marry.

"Did he propose to you?" she asked.

"No, he doesn't know about this—well, not yet."

But within minutes of our conversation, the phone rang. I picked up the receiver, and there he was. I made pointing gestures to Judy and silently mouthed, "It's him, it's him!"

I played it cool when he asked if I remembered him and played it even cooler when he asked if I'd be at Cyril's party.

"I'm not sure," I said, and then just in case he changed his mind, I coyly said, "I'll go if you go."

And with that we agreed to meet there. I couldn't wait for Saturday. Of course, I needed a new dress—something black—but then thinking of him I figured I should be more demure than sexy, so I decided not to buy a dress, as I had one that I wore on the ship and instead purchased a gorgeous pair of four-inch black patent heel shoes and night shade nylons. Simple and elegant. I spent extra time on my makeup and hair. I wanted him to notice me and remember me.

Cyril had a car call for me, and when I arrived, I looked around for Sydney. He wasn't there. I tried to cover my disappointment by lighting a cigarette. He arrived fashionably late—I have to tell you I was almost in despair—in a dark dinner jacket, completely alone. We made eye contact, and I waited for him to come over. It seemed like forever before he joined me. You have to understand that back then men had to make the first move—there was no way I would walk over to him and start up a conversation. So just imagine how I felt while he took his time small talking with different people. Finally he came over and we went off to a corner to talk. I have no idea what we spoke about yet I still remember the tingle of excitement that swept right through me. I had never felt this way about anyone before. Sydney suggestively remarked on how dull the whole party was and recommended that we leave. I didn't need a second invitation. We quietly sneaked out and drove away. We went to Ginsberg's Casablanca, a drive-in diner and forever afterwards my favorite place. We ordered coffee. The waitress clipped our tray onto the window, and we never stopped talking. When the diner closed, Sydney drove to a spot that overlooked Johannesburg, and like the perfect gentleman that he was, he asked me if he could hold my hand. I had never met anyone like him, nor had I ever spoken so deeply before about my life. I know I must have told him a great deal about my life—not everything that night, but almost all of it—and he told me *almost* everything about him. Almost because I was in for a few surprises. After what seemed like a few hours, I asked him, "What is that peculiar light?" He looked around and with a sweet smile replied, "That, young lady, is the dawn breaking." We had spent the whole night together talking.

From that day on, we were never apart. Still, a couple of surprises were in the offing. I think it was probably a few weeks after we met when we drove up to a friend's house who was having a party. As we entered, the host stopped us outside and said, "I just have to warn you that my children have the chicken pox."

I took two steps forward—I'd had it ages ago—but Sydney hung back. "Sorry, I can't come in," he said. "I have two little boys who might catch it."

This small bombshell exploded in my head. I was shaken, speechless. He had never mentioned that he was married or that he had children. Sydney must have seen my face because he grabbed my arm and hastily led me back to his car. I demanded that he take me home. "I was going to tell you," he said. "I am divorced and have custody of my two boys, Rodney, who is four, and Darryl, who is two and half years old."

I was flabbergasted and angry because I felt deceived. He then continued to tell me that he was a struggling musician living in a very small house with his mother and father and the children. "I supplement my wages by making suitcases and jigsaw puzzles and every day, when I'm not building them, I'm trying to sell them. I work very hard making sure that I make enough to support my family. Last year I had it all. I owned two night clubs, a mansion in Lower Houghton—the best suburb in Johannesburg—and then like a house of cards everything crashed and I lost everything. All I have left is this pair of hands, a few good suits, and my wits. I know I can make anything and will never allow my family to starve. Things may be tough now, but we'll swing through this and really start living again. If you want to stay around I can't offer or promise you anything. But if you do stay, I can assure you will be one we will be one fantastic team."

Whatever I had felt for Sydney now trebled, and I was even more hopelessly in love with him. He was my hero and I—I was going to be his *'knightingale'* in shining armour. I knew I could rescue him together we would live happily ever after!

I didn't have a fortune, but I had saved quite a tidy sum of money that I brought with me to South Africa. This was my security. If I was unhappy or if things didn't work out, I knew I could always return or if it took me longer than anticipated to get a job, I knew I'd be able to survive independently from Ann. While Ann was a wonderful, caring sister, I never wanted to take advantage of our relationship.

Without a second thought, I started to make plans to use this to help Sydney and the boys. I moved into a larger apartment, purchased clothes for Rodney and Darryl, and whenever I visited the house I arrived with a huge parcel of groceries. My nest egg decreased very quickly, yet I was not concerned, as professionally I was doing very well. I was promoted to "Traveller." This position came with a driver, as I had to call on the shops and department stores around the perimeter of Johannesburg. Without realizing it, the connections I made at this time would serve me very well when I started my company, Elizabeth Grant.

I took Sydney' s jigsaw puzzles and suitcases with me on every trip and always sold the lot. I hoped he'd appreciate me more and marry me soon. This was my plan—not his—but being very determined, I usually got what I wanted.

Sydney was highly cerebral, not the sort of man who allowed emotions to rule him. But as the months went on, I remember saying to him, "Sometimes you have to let your heart rule your head. We love one another—what more do you want?"He was sixteen years older than me and was also was very stern, cold, and implacable. He was brilliant and at times, very funny. He was fluent in German; he played music beautifully, and he read voraciously. When he lived in London he ran a highly successful interior decorating company. The Prince of Wales and Mrs. Wallace Simpson commissioned him to decorate their apartment. He was innovative with his designs and won many awards for his furniture designs. Like most young lovers, I worshipped his feet. His every utterance was important. I drank it all in like a willing pupil.

All I ever spoke about to friends and family was, "Sydney says this, Sydney thinks that," which Ann found irritating and said so. "It's enough. I'm sick and tired about hearing all these accolades—come back to earth," Ann moaned.

He plied me with his vast knowledge and personal opinions at every turn. Like Professor Henry Higgins, he wanted his "Eliza" to expand both her enunciation and vocabulary. He'd give me a new word to learn every day.

I remember the first time I heard "tintinnabulation"— now, there's a word! He also taught me musical composition, quarter notes and the like, and which chords were sad and why. I had to become quite expert on musical instruments, opera, ballet, and other cultural pursuits, even if I didn't have a great affinity for them.

Early in our relationship I'd told him about my secret serum. One day while we were arguing because I thought he was taking too long to produce his puzzles it hit me—why don't we make up the serum and sell it? I thought we were the perfect team, and I said to him, "I can't do it alone." I suppose this finally pulled some of those emotions to the surface because he replied, "I think you have a winner here—I'll take care of everything. I know a chemist, I'll design the label." Sydney was excited. I couldn't get him to marry me, but he was interested in doing business.

Fortunately, the manager of my building decided the issue of marriage for us. Apparently there was a census being done locally, and now I had to let him know exactly how many people were living in my flat. So I told Sydney about it, and he (never the romantic) replied, "Well, we may as well get married." I didn't need a second invitation. I phoned Mummy to tell her the good news that finally the love of my life who I'd been writing about all this time had proposed and we were getting married. "Just remember what I told you," she said. I remember putting down the receiver and smiling—I was in love and it was a wonderful feeling. We married in 1948 in a civil ceremony at the Registrar's office.

Whatever else I might have had to face, whatever surprises, good or bad, it didn't matter. I was married to the man of my dreams. I trusted him and knew that he wouldn't let me down. I liked the way he looked admiringly at me. He often sought out my opinions, and he treated me with respect. Remember, I had been raised on a steady diet of rejection; I was told how ugly I was, how no man would ever want me. Sydney was much older than I, sixteen years my senior, and so dashing and brilliant. For such a man to make me his wife—I was more than temporarily smitten. I was absolutely besotted!

I often parallel my falling in love with Sydney with my mother's relationship with Isaac. When I met Sydney, I knew that was it. He was everything I wanted and made excuses for everything and anything that was not right. I discounted the fact that he hadn't been forthright about his children, that he didn't have a proper job and was barely making enough to support his family. I was in love, and somehow this seemed to conquer all.

My mother did the same when she met Isaac. He was unemployed, divorced with five children, and penniless. She fell in love with him the moment he walked into her restaurant and never stopped to think how this could impact her life. She believed that she could make everything right, and then, like all good fairy tales, they would live happily ever after. But as we all know, life is not a fairy tale, and there are no magic wands. Mummy's attempt to put everything right resulted in her losing everything—her fortune, her family, and most important of all, her independence. That was what she tried to tell me when we last met.

Yet at the time I failed to see the parallel because love is blind. I am not decrying my love, nor have I ever regretted my decision to marry, but I believe I could have managed this better. My decision to rescue Sydney changed the dynamic, and once the course is altered there's no going back. Our relationship became one of dependence that on reflection negatively impacted on our family life. In our marriage my sole purpose was to keep Sydney secure. He and the business were was always first—the children followed, not in second place, but were placed last. But more of this in another chapter.

Dressed for shopping

Preparing for a show

Modelling first fur coat

Modelling Hats

Elizabeth with friend

CHAPTER 9

BUILDING A BUSINESS, 1950–1990

I am always asked what motivated me to start a business in a time when this was essentially a man's world and the answer is simply I had to make ends meet.

In London I wanted to earn extra money and needed to save for the trip to South Africa. In Johannesburg, selling serum seemed easier than making and selling jigsaw puzzles and suitcases. In the beginning I never realized I was starting a business. It was just a way to supplement my income and make life easier for my instant family. Whatever I earned I gave to Sydney. This afforded us a really comfortable flat and a better lifestyle.

A few years after my son, Paul, was born, I knew it was time. Elizabeth Grant Skincare had the potential to be a big business, and I sat down with Sydney to plan the future of the company. Sydney recommended that we meet with a business developer who could help us structure the business and advise us on the business. This made sense to me, and we made an appointment. I have to admit I was a bit nervous—this was a big step. I changed outfits at least four times and eventually settled on a plain black dress and low black patent pumps.

We were ushered into his office and sat opposite his mahogany desk. Sydney did most of the talking. He explained that I had a brilliant serum that was gaining popularity and we wanted to develop this further, expand the product line, and sell the brand internationally.

"What capital do you have to support this?" he asked. Without flinching, Sydney replied that we had strong interest from an investor, which is why we were now seriously considering launching the brand. Whether he believed us or not, I'll never forget his reply. He was from the States and with an American drawl he asked, "Have you got a million dollars? That's what you'll need start a cosmetic business *big time* today." I'd had enough of this game and stood up and I told him it was ridiculous. Any fool could start a business with a million dollars—and blow a million dollars very quickly. We were going to start small and make it on our own. I heard him say, "Yeah right" as we left his office. I was a little annoyed with Sydney for being pretentious and going back in the car I wrote some simple points down in my notebook:

1. Register company
2. Go to bank—bank account and cheque book
3. Create full system—cleanser, toner, serum, day cream, night cream, mask for all skin types
4. Arrange terms with factory
5. Sydney to design logo and leaflets
6. Use stock bottles and jars (NB, don't spend a million dollars)
7. Colors white and gold—high luxury (make it look like a million dollars)
8. Visit fashion buyers in the country and ascertain cosmetic buyer's name., Give serum to each buyer
9. Get into stores.

Now I had my plan clearly defined, and I knew that whatever happened I would be in the stores. I shared this with Sydney, and we were so excited. This was it.

I met with the chemist, and together we formulated the full line of skincare products. Each product had my compound Torricelumn ™. This took quite a while, as every product was tested, but I didn't care how long it took. It was like preparing for a new baby. Every spare moment I had I raced to the lab to touch, feel, and smell. My skin was very sensitive, making me the perfect guinea pig. Once I gave it the go ahead we then tested each product on thirty women—different ages and different skin types.

Sydney arranged to incorporate the company, opened the bank account ,and received a chequebook that had Elizabeth Grant International Inc. imprinted on each cheque. Receiving the first cheque book was quite moving, and I, who always cries at the drop of a hat, felt my eyes well up with tears until Sydney said in an exasperated tone, "For goodness sake, Elizabeth, don't be so silly."

This may surprise you, but I had never owned a cheque book, and to see my name (albeit the name of the company) written on the top left hand side of every cheque was as exciting, I should imagine, as seeing my name up in lights! I asked Sydney to show me how to write a cheque and he said, "Darling, it's not really a good idea for business reasons. I'd explain, but it's very complicated, and you wouldn't understand."

Of course, this didn't make sense, but I was more interested in developing and selling the products and I let this go. Later this decision would haunt me, because giving up financial control was probably the most serious mistake I ever made in business. I just didn't realize it at the time.

I like to share this lesson, as it is always easy to give away rights at the start of a project because when you have nothing you can't conceive the full impact of what you are doing. I trusted Sydney, and that was enough. But being in business involves having a keen understanding of what is being spent and what is coming in—expenses and income. Never let anyone take this right away from you.

Admittedly, I had hoped Sydney would step in when it came to the nitty-gritty of day-to-day operations—this really wasn't my area of interest. And true to his word, he did so with a formidable vigor. He thrived on running things—the negotiations, the orders and shipments, the financial planning and expansions. I was grateful for that. I was free to sell, to discuss product development, to open new doors.

The trouble was that once Sydney took control of the business, he also took more control of me.

Like many of his peers, he kept his hands on the purse strings and dictated the budget. I—of all women—who had practically raised myself, who had supported myself since the age of thirteen, found myself chafing against this and a multitude of other constraints. I was not unlike a wild stallion feeling penned in and wanting to buck anyone who tried to tame me.

It was very, very hard, believe me. Sydney gave me a monthly allowance. This made sense in the beginning as we were building together—but he never wanted to increase this, and you can imagine how humiliated I felt every time I had to ask him for something. I had free rein over the domestic aspects at home. But beyond that, I felt like the "adornment," a figurehead, leaving the house with a handbag that held a comb, tissue, a lipstick, the keys to the front door—and not much else. No money of consequence.

Discussions and scenarios went something like this.

"Sydney? Tell me about our shipping operation."

"You wouldn't understand it, darling—it's too complicated."

"Sydney, I was thinking I could use a typewriter—"

"Darling, too complicated."

"Look, I need to learn to drive a car—"

"Are you mad? With your temperament, you'd probably kill somebody."

"Sydney, dear, I'd like to open my own cheque account … I *need* a cheque account."

"Much too complicated for you, darling, and not good for business—for tax reasons I'll explain another time."

One day I decided to take the reins in my own hand and went into a bank to open my own account.

Remembering my mother's advice from all those years ago, I made up my mind that it was time to start building my own little nest egg. But in those days the banks required my husband to sign the application form. I was incensed and demanded to see the bank manager, who rather imperiously came over and merely reiterated what the bank clerk had said.

Sydney was a Victorian husband in a modern world, and I enabled this both at home and in business by pretending that it didn't matter.

Initially I kept my sales job to help supplement the income and we worked from home. The products were made at an external factory. Sydney collected them and stored them in the store room of our apartment. Monday to Thursday I worked at my sales job and Friday to Sunday were the EG days. I met with customers, planned "beauty parties," and took orders which, when I got home, we'd go down to the storeroom together to pack up the orders, which I always delivered the next week. From my experience I knew that quick, personal deliveries were part of good customer service. It was hard work and very hands on. In those early days our customers were individuals and small stores. It was very difficult to break into the larger department stores. Yet I still called on them as often as possible, leaving samples with whoever I met. Every month we were able to cover expenses, but it was tough going, and there was very little extra. Yet at no stage did I ever think of giving up; I concentrated on building it up.

One afternoon I called home to speak to Sydney and he didn't answer the phone. I was concerned and called back every twenty minutes. Eventually the maid answered the phone.

"Where's Sydney?" I asked.
"He's sleeping," she replied.
I wondered if he was sick, and when I arrived home I asked him if he was feeling well. "Never better, my darling."

"Then why were you sleeping this afternoon?" I asked.
"I often have an afternoon nap," he replied.

I felt as though I had been slapped in the face. I was working two jobs, day and night, on a measly allowance while he was at home napping. Something was definitely wrong with the picture. I was so frustrated I went to Ann and then got mad with her when she said, "I told you so."

For the first time in my life I started to feel trapped. I had no money, and my business had not grown as fast as I envisioned. It had been over ten years, and it was still nowhere close to where it should have been. I needed a plan.

Mummy had taught me with all serious matters not to be impetuous, as this inevitably leads to bad decisions. She learned this from her firsthand disastrous experiences with the restaurant and hotel business. Once again I took her advice. I took a sheet of paper, drew a line down the middle, and on the one side I wrote the word "plus" and on the other side I wrote the word "minus." Mummy always said if there were more minuses than plusses, drastic action was necessary.

It's an amazing thing when you put pen to paper. First of all, it definitely makes you think differently. Years later I showed this to my son, Paul. He explained that this exercise takes one away from making emotional decisions, as it helps center the brain on a more rational and logical line. This reiterated what I have always known about my mother. She had no education, couldn't read or write, she never mastered English—yet she was incredibly perceptive and had the wisdom of Solomon.

I looked at the list I wrote about Sydney, the plusses were all there. As a husband and father, he was everything I wanted. As a business partner, there were attributes that I needed—definite leadership and organizational skills. He knew about

SYDNEY		
	PLUS	MINUS-
1	ARTISITC	GETS BORED EASILY
2	GOOD LEADER	DEMANDING
3	HARDWORKING	SLEEPS IN AFTERNOON?
4	GOOD FATHER	BIT MEAN
5	ENTREPREURING	DISCIPLINARIAN—LIKE A SCHOOLMASTER
6	INTERESTING	
7	LOYAL	
8	FAIR MINDED	
9	GOOD SENSE OF HUMOUR	
10	NEVER HITS ME	
11	GOOD TO THE CHILDREN	
12	LOVES ANIMALS	
13	CLEVER	
14	NEVER DULL	

ELIZABETH GRANT SKINCARE		
	PLUS+	MINUS-
1	PRODUCT WORKS	TOUGH IN SOUTH AFRICA–SEVEN YEARS
2	VERY LOYAL CUSTOMERS	
3	SUCCESSFUL IN LONDON	
4.	LONDON –TWO YEARS	

book keeping. He could type. He was very creative—easily bored but certainly creative. That's probably why he had taken to napping. He was well connected and had a distinguished aplomb that men respected at meetings. This was important, as business then was definitely a man's world. He added an assertive voice at meetings.

When I looked at the list on EG, it made me realize that the business was more successful in London in two years than I had been in South Africa in seven years. My leaving London, while a great personal decision, was probably one of the worst business decisions I had made at the time. I made up my mind that it was time to go back to London. I've always been the sort of person that once I make my mind up about something, I initiate it very quickly. I would have to persuade Sydney that going back to London was a brilliant idea, and I knew that in order to get his commitment, I'd have to have a very strong case. Sydney had just celebrated his fiftieth birthday, and the older he got the more set in his ways he became. He wouldn't be partial to selling up and moving the family back to London unless he really agreed with me that this would be in our best interests—totally.

How could I guarantee the success of Elizabeth Grant?

What could I do to ensure financial security for the family?

Where would we live?

What would we live on while building the business?

Who could help us?

I took out my British client list I had kept all those years in my "Scrap Box of Memories," as I called it. I remember when I placed the list there. I almost threw it out as it took up so much space, but then I put it back again because a little voice in my head said, "Elizabeth you never know." (Thank you, Papa.) Looking at the list of names, I drafted this letter that I personalized to each client.

Dear Client,

This is Elizabeth Grant calling. Guess what? I hope to be seeing you very shortly, as I am returning to London in November this year.

I remember how you just loved our serums. We are currently extending the line and will be offering a total skincare routine and every product contains my Torricelumn.

When we last met it was at an Elizabeth Grant party that you kindly hosted at your home. I remember the delicious biscuits you made for tea. I thank you again. I am planning on doing the same upon my return. As my diary is filling up rapidly, please write back and let me know etc.

I posted these letters and prayed.

I also wrote to my brother Ralph enlisting his help. I asked him if he could find work for Sydney and accommodation for the family. Within a couple of weeks he replied and said this was perfect timing as he needed a manager to oversee his dress factory. With regard to accommodation, he would make arrangements for an apartment in his building. I was absolutely thrilled, and I called Ralph to thank him profusely.

I also started to get a lot of replies from my *Torricelumn*™ *Girls*. Their response made me very emotional. I got a bit weepy—I laughed—I cried—I was very joyful. I just knew this was the right thing to do.

Before I went further with this, I decided to seek some professional help and went to our accountant. What I wanted to know was whether this was a good business decision, what we would need to earn to maintain financial security, and what was needed to fund the business in London. What would it take?

We went over the figures. He calculated that Sydney's income would more than cover the rent and living expenses. If I did a minimum of three parties a week, the business would be profitable.

Now armed with all this information, I approached Sydney. I spread everything out in front of him and said, "Sydney, this is a golden opportunity. We have a home waiting for us. You have a job tailor made for you, and I'm going to take up where I left off. You cannot say no to this proposition."

My excitement filtered through to him, and he agreed.

Within a month I sold up everything and had our air tickets to London. I wrote back to my *Torricelumn™ Girls* and brought their appointments forward.

We packed and shipped out all the Elizabeth Grant stock so I could start up immediately when I arrived. The boys were so excited. They all had new clothes, and I was champing at the bit. I couldn't wait to get back to London.

We arrived at Heathrow, but my brother was not there to meet us. I phoned the factory. His secretary answered and put me through to him. I said, "Hello." He said, "Yes?"
"It's me, Elizabeth!"
"Elizabeth who?"

I started to get a knot in my stomach, as I felt that something was not quite right.
"It's your sister—we're at Heathrow."

He asked me to put Sydney on the phone and gave him directions to his house.

We piled into a taxi and were warmly welcomed by Marie, Ralph's wife. She made us all a nice cup of tea, true English style, with sandwiches and cakes. After tea I asked Marie for the keys to our flat, as we were all tired and needed to unpack.

"What flat?" she said.

"What do you mean, 'what flat?' The flat that Ralph arranged for us. It's furnished. He told us he arranged it," I said.

She laughed and in a questioning voice asked, "You take notice of your crazy brother?"

One thing I always admired abut Sydney was his calm, precise way of taking everything in his stride. When I panicked he'd say to me, "Is there anything you can do about this at this precise moment?" And I'd say, "No." Then he'd say, "Well, there you are. We will sit down calmly, rationalize it, and then do the right thing. Panic does not enter into this discussion. Once you panic you've lost it. We will work things out to our best interests."

I was panic stricken. It seemed as though in my effort to get back to London I had jeopardized everything. I had uprooted the whole family and persuaded Sydney to leave South Africa at a time in his life when it wasn't easy to start again. I had always known that my brother was an irresponsible lout, but I ignored this because his offer to help was critical to "*The Plan.*" In my quest to have everything planned for our return, I had blotted this out.

Sydney took me aside and said, "It's been a long day. Tomorrow we'll look at our options." What a way to start our new venture! Of course, when Ralph eventually breezed in, he told us not to worry—he would take care of everything. We'd stay with him until everything was sorted out, and Sydney should go with him to the factory the next day. He was delighted that Sydney had arrived so soon, as he was in desperate need of a factory manager. I needed to trust him, but there was a nagging doubt tapping inside me every time he spoke.

That night I looked at Sydney and broke down. Talk about the end of a very long day. Our trip to London was exhausting. My brother had let us down. We had no apartment. I was scared that the job Ralph promised wouldn't materialize. Sydney put his arm around me and told me not to worry. We had a roof over our heads—albeit Ralph's house—and he had a job. "Elizabeth, everything will work out. Don't give up your dream."

Sydney started to work for Ralph and within three months had the factory running smoothly and more efficiently. Production increased by almost 100 percent. But true to my brother's character, Sydney never received the salary he had been offered, and one day he walked out in utter frustration.

We took our own apartment. I contacted Charles, who recommended me to a factory. I started to organize parties, and this kept us going. The boys went to the local school. Mummy and Isaac came from Glasgow to visit us. Our reunion was wonderful. They adored the boys.

As I have always maintained, out of bad comes good. The day that Sydney walked out of the factory Charles called us and said he wanted us to meet two brothers, Morris and Douglas, who were looking to invest in a skincare line. This was a perfect opportunity. Sydney and I met them, and I felt they had the potential to expand our business in a big way. They were well connected in the beauty world and had contacts in salons that extended out of London to Manchester, Leeds, Liverpool, and in Europe to Paris and Rome. I felt that once again luck was on my side.

We took premises opposite the Tate Gallery. Sydney took over the administration again. Morris and Douglas were not really involved in the day-to-day running of the business— they were silent partners, but their contribution was enormous. They made me think bigger. They got us orders from salons all over England and Paris and Rome and suddenly the company took on an international flavor—London, Rome, Paris. Sydney put this on the labels of all our products. I moved away from parties and started to call on salons in and around London. My goal was still landing a major store.

One day I in was in Selfridges, the biggest store in London, and on the spur of the moment I decided to go and see the buyers. I had my samples with me and asked a salesperson in the beauty department where the buyer was. To my amazement, I learned that the buying department was in a separate building behind Selfridges. She also advised me to make an appointment, as they never saw anyone without one. Undeterred, I walked over, knocked on the door, and marched in to be greeted by two astonished-looking, middle-aged ladies.

Without waiting, I sat down and said, "Please give me a hearing. I have something I want to tell you."

I proceeded to tell them my story about the bomb blast and my discovery of Torricelumn™. I then opened my bag and gave each buyer a sample and said, "Try it and call me back if you're interested."

One of the buyers asked me to leave my card. Card? I had never had a card, but I didn't want them to think I was unprofessional, so without hesitating I replied, "I don't have one with me. Here is my phone number, call me if you're interested."

Within a week the phone rang. It was Selfridges. I was overwhelmed to hear the buyer say, "How soon can you come and see us?"

This was in some ways my finest hour. Sydney and I worked together on this project. I impressed the buyers with my line, and Sydney closed the deal.

The day Elizabeth Grant Skincare debuted at Selfridges, I was absolutely astounded to discover they had given me the entrance and front window displays. I couldn't believe my luck. I had never been happier. And what's more, we had two prime counter locations when you walked in. I trained the beauty consultants, and we kept emptying our shelves like it was Christmas—it was crazy. It had taken me ten long, hard years to arrive at Selfridges.

Two facts stand out. The first is that hard work, perseverance, and determination takes you where you want to go and the second, there is no looking back.

From 1958 to the present, Elizabeth Grant Skincare has remained a beauty empire founded on the discovery of a most remarkable essence, Torricelumn™.

The success of Selfridges opened the door to other stores, and soon we were in Whitely's and the Army and Navy Stores. The beauty editor of *Vogue Magazine* called and asked to see me and gave us a fabulous write up. We were well on our way and then a bombshell. Sydney called me into his office, asked me to sit down as he had something very important to discuss with me. He was terribly unhappy in London and wanted to go back to South Africa. He hated the weather. He had no friends and longed for South Africa. I was flabbergasted. I never dreamed he felt like this. We had purchased a flat in Bayswater, had a two-year lease on office premises, plus our business was so successful. It didn't make sense that he would want to leave. My fear was what would happen to EG. I voiced this, and Sydney assured me that Morris and Douglas could manage the UK account very well and he went on to say, "We have our flat here, so there's nothing to stop us from coming back here every three months or so to check on everything. We will be in constant touch with them by phone."

I always worked very hard at making my marriage successful, but this was a difficult moment I can tell you. On the one hand, Elizabeth Grant was the most wonderful accomplishment of my life. On the other hand, Sydney and the boys were also of prime importance. What was I to do? I asked Sydney to give me couple of days to consider this

Mulling it over the idea of returning to South Arica became appealing. I thought armed with our UK success, the South African department stores would be more receptive to EG. This was an opportunity for international expansion.

I had to be confident that our partners would be able to manage, and I asked Sydney to arrange a meeting with them, preferably on a Saturday, which meant no interruptions. I wanted to be assured that without us being in London, they would make Elizabeth Grant a top priority and continue the high volume of success that we had accomplished.

But Sydney met them on his own.

I had been on an appointment with the buyer from Selfridges who gave me our biggest order ever. I raced back to the office to tell Sydney (because in those days we didn't have cell phones). As I opened the door, Sydney said, "Darling, we have nothing to be concerned about. I met with *the boys*" (this was our pet name for them) "and they assured me they will run it as though we were still here."

I was dismayed that Sydney hadn't bothered to do what I asked him and that was to have the meeting together over the weekend. I hated it when he discounted my needs. I still had an unsettling niggle in my stomach. While our partners were well connected and had opened many doors for us, Elizabeth Grant was only one of their many investments, and they had never worked at EG full time. I procured all the orders. I was in the stores every day training the staff, meeting with the buyers, and planning the new products. Many a day I went into a store and worked behind the counters to boost sales. For me EG was my whole life and a simple assurance from Sydney that "*the boys*" knew what to do didn't make me feel good. I wanted to know what their plan was—this I never got. I was so frustrated and we started to argue. When I insisted that he set up another meeting, he told me to stop worrying and tried to reassure me over and over again, "You're not talking about irresponsible men. They're not idiots. You're talking about hugely successful businessmen." The more I protested, the more he continued. He challenged me with, "Don't you trust me? Have I ever failed you? You know I'd never let you down and never do anything injurious to EG."

Finally he convinced me. I called Mummy and told her we were going back to South Africa. I shared my concerns and in her wise way she said, "Sometimes it's not easy to understand why men do what they do. They like to think that they're the boss. Go back to South Africa with your husband, let him think he's the boss when you start up the business again. But this time keep control over the money and you'll be fine." She promised to visit us when we were settled.

We went back by boat, and the three boys had the time of their lives. We sailed out of England on a dreary day and then two days out to sea, the sun was shining, the weather was warm, and I have to tell you this had a magical effect on me. I felt good. Sydney and I spent a lot of time talking and planning. The more he talked, the more confident I felt. We were at sea for two weeks—this was like our first "holiday" together. We laughed, played, danced, and I fell deeply in love again. Sydney was still very dashing, and at night when we dressed for dinner, I felt proud when he slipped his arm through mine and escorted me to the table.

"You don't have a care in the world. Leave everything to me." Once again, without heeding Mummy's words, I did.

My first task, after the family had settled in Johannesburg, was to make appointments with the buyers from the major stores.

The first major hurdle in any business is landing the first account. I decided to go after Greatermans, as they had several stores in all the major cities in South Africa. Their head office was in Johannesburg, where we lived. Sydney felt I was being a both impetuous and presumptuous and suggested that I start with the smaller stores. Fortunately, I didn't listen to this, and I called and made an appointment to meet the beauty buyer . I asked Sydney to design an EG cosmetic case to hold our samples. When it came to creativity, he was brilliant. He made a navy blue cosmetic case emblazoned with our gold logo. The he put together an EG portfolio with our product line, brochures, and write ups.

For the appointment I wore a plain navy dress, a matching blazer with gold buttons, and black patent leather shoes. The only jewelry I wore was a pearl necklace—sophisticated chic.

Upon meeting the buyer I realized she was a Londoner. Talk about luck. I read her name on her desk and it struck a bell and I asked her, "What's your mother and father's first name?" When she told me I sat back in the chair and said, "You're not going to believe this, but I know your Mum and Dad." We laughed. Immediately we had a common bond. Although heritage alone doesn't make a deal, it certainly helps to break the ice. I showed her our line of products, took out the portfolio, and told her about our success in London.

I could see she was impressed—both with the products and my enthusiasm. I told her how I had helped shape the success of the brand in London with my hands-on help. I would do the same here—train the consultants, call on them regularly, even work the counters when necessary. We could hold "Meet Elizabeth Grant Events." Our meeting lasted well over an hour, and I left with our first purchase order from a South African department store with the one proviso—she wanted me to work the counter for the first month. She gave us a counter in the city center. This was their largest store. How well this went would determine which other stores she would place us in.

Two weeks later I called her, only to be told that she had been transferred to Cape Town. Once again I knew my Papa was looking after me. If I had waited like Sydney recommended, I would have missed out on a golden opportunity.

On learning of this coup, Sydney flew into immediate action. First, he secured a manufacturer with prior experience in cosmetics. I designed a line of products to include bath and body treatments.

I worked relentlessly. This was probably to the detriment of my family—the boys would ask, "Where's Mummy?" and they'd hear, "She's working," or "She had to go out of town," but the truth is, I've never regretted it because I was doing the job I was put here to do.

We set up offices for Elizabeth Grant,and we hit the ground running. There was no stopping me. I went to each and every major store in Johannesburg and took orders. We were off to a flying start. Once again Sydney took over the administration and finances. I was in charge of sales, sales staff, and growing the business.

We advertised for staff, and after I interviewed them, I sent them home with the products that they had to use for one week. My staff had to love the products and love what they were doing if they wanted to work with me.

I often found myself selling alongside the beauty consultants, with enormous success. I trained them ahead of taking their positions and on the job as well.

In addition to training new sales staff locally, I had to travel to Durban and Cape Town as, one by one, store branches began to carry the Elizabeth Grant line. At the same time, I was still knocking on new doors.

It took me six years to get the buyer at Belfast to see me. Six years! But I never stopped calling, each and every week. I simply worked nonstop.

When videotape replaced the old kinescope, it made sense to videotape the training techniques and send them round to the various locations for the staff. Sydney built a television studio, complete with closed-circuit video tape recording cameras, and made training films for the staff. In many ways he was ahead of his time and later on he started one of the first video in-house training schools.

The years were rolling by, and the company was growing. Business overseas was steady. I was always a bit disappointed with its slow growth and was convinced that had I been there we would by now have seen at least a triple-figure growth, but Sydney assured me that steady business was good business. In South Africa we were doing splendidly. I had my own chauffeured car, exquisite jewelry, fur coats, and a lovely home, and then, suddenly, everything changed.

Sydney complained that he wasn't feeling well. I made an appointment with our doctor, but he refused to go. "I'll be fine," he said. He hated going to the doctor; he thought ill health it was a sign of weakness. One night he collapsed in pain. I called our house doctor, who rushed over, examined him, and immediately booked him into hospital. It was late at night, and he asked me to call him once Sydney was checked in, irrespective of the time. The specialist examined him the next morning and told me he suspected a blockage and had to operate. Sydney looked so frail I started to get fearful. Ann, who was with me, led me to the waiting room.

I remember her saying, "Whatever happens, you have to be brave," But I, who was so strong about so many things, have never coped well with illness. While waiting I bit my nails and picked the skin off my fingertips. Try as hard as I could to tackle this logically, sensibly, bravely—this was impossible. In business I was strong. When things go wrong with my family, I become an emotional wreck and can't cope. A clear example is when the doctor came to give me the results of the operation I blocked out everything he said. What he *told* me was that he had removed a cancerous tumour—what I *heard* was Sydney was going to be okay. When I joyfully told Ann that Sydney was going to be fine, she gave me a peculiar look and then put her arms around me and hugged me tightly. We never mentioned cancer again.

While Sydney was in the hospital, I worked from the office. I wanted to be close to the hospital in case I was needed. But fate had another reason for me being there.

The phone rang, and a rather irate voice asked to speak to Sydney.

"He's not in," I explained. He was in hospital recovering from an operation.

"Well I hope you can help me," he continued. "I need payment on this account. You are four months behind, and we will not deliver any more products until such time as I receive payment."

"There must be some misunderstanding," I said. "Sydney manages all this, and he won't be back for a least a month."

"I cannot extend your credit," he said. "I have been calling Sydney for over two months now—I'm tired of hearing that this will be taken care of. Until I receive payment, your account is suspended. Nothing will be delivered."

I hung up the phone. At first I was so angry. How dare he call me like this when Sydney had been so sick! Then I started to worry—why hadn't Sydney paid the account? The business was doing very well. I certainly knew this from the orders I brought in. Then a nagging suspicion worked its way to the pit of my stomach, and I started to shake. What was going on? I unlocked Sydney's office, went to the cupboard where the books were kept, and looked at the figures. Nothing made sense. I took a deep breath and called the accountant. I briefly told him what had happened. "I need you to come over right away. I can't stop my heart from pounding, and I'm really scared."

He must have heard my voice, because he arrived at the office within the hour.

In a nutshell, I learned that the business was bankrupt. How? Why? What happened? How long he spent with me I truly don't know. Exactly what he said I couldn't tell you either. All I remember was hearing snippets of words with the one pervading sentence constantly banging inside my head.

"We're bankrupt—it's over."
"Morris's wife died." Why are we bankrupt?
Lost interest ... how could this happen?
No follow up ... what will I do?
Sydney pumped money into London ... where is all the money?
Rent had to be paid ... it can't be over.
Partners need money ... We're bankrupt—it's over.
Sydney had let me down. I thought back to everything—
"Sydney can I have a chequebook?"
"Darling, you wouldn't understand. It's too complicated."

In London after meeting Morris and Douglas without me—"You're not talking about irresponsible men. They're not idiots. You're talking about hugely successful businessmen. Trust me. I'll never let you down. We'll make one hell-of a team."

And while all this noise was going on in my head, the loudest voice was my mother's, "Always keep control of the money."

I was shattered, in shock, totally numbed. As much as I blamed Sydney for this mess inwardly, over and over again I asked, "How could I have allowed this to happen?"

I thought back to the measly allowance he gave me—the furs and jewelry he purchased. Were they paid for? I realized why he hadn't taken me to London this past year. "Darling, you're too busy. Stay here and I'll pop over to prop things up."

When the accountant finally stopped speaking, I looked at him quietly for a short while, took in a few deep breaths, and said, "Very simply—advise me. What do I need to do?"

He closed the accounting book, looked away, and said, "The easiest route is for the business to declare bankruptcy. This will give the business time to pay back debts or restructure its debt or have most of the debts absolved completely. This is the advice I gave Sydney months ago, but he didn't listen. He kept on saying, 'Stop worrying—it will come right.' But I must warn you, declaring bankruptcy is a public announcement, and this will jeopardize your position at the stores. They have the right to ask you to leave."

"Do it," I said. "Restructure the debt. I will ensure that all our creditors are paid—with the exception of Morris and Douglas. They must responsible for their mess." I told him to work with our lawyer and dissolve the partnership.

Like a house of cards, everything crumbled—and so quickly. One day I had it all—the next day debt collectors surrounded me, grabbing everything and anything of value.

Losing the stores was heart wrenching. I had worked so hard to establish our position, but I adopted the stoic attitude my mother had all those years ago. I refused to look back put all my energy into surviving one day at a time. *"Get on with it. Move forward."* My focus was how to protect the family, rebuild the company, and restore the good name of Elizabeth Grant. This was why I told our accountant that I wouldn't have the debt absolved. Rather, I would make a plan to ensure that everyone was paid back. This was a huge commitment—it would not be easy, but there was no other option.

I made the decision not to discuss this with Sydney while he was in hospital. This was impossibly difficult and many a day I couldn't visit him because it was so hard to pretend. By the time he was discharged, I was more than ready—I was prepared. The why it happened was no longer important. What really mattered was how we were going to get it right.

When he arrived home I took him to the dining room. The accounting books were on the table, which he noticed immediately. He started to stammer our a few words, "Darling I didn't ..." When I interrupted him, "Sydney, I know everything. Don't say a word. For too many years I've allowed you to control everything. This stops now. From this point forward we will do things my way."

I had my jewelry appraised and negotiated a fair price for the lot, and whatever I could sell that had any value was marked to go. I calculated this would allow us to survive for a few months.

The fact that we'd lost the stores was a done deal. But, and this is what had kept me going, we hadn't lost our clients. From the day I started the business, all those years ago in London, I kept an updated client list. Luckily I'd been able to retrieve stock from some of the stores, which I estimated would last two months, and I went to the factory to make arrangements for extended credit.

I've always said that there are two kinds of meetings—the buying and the selling. When you're buying, the supplier fawns over you. Brings you coffee. Takes his time. Makes you promises. When you're selling, you don't get coffee. You have to make the promise. And you're the one on a time clock *unless* you are able to turn what you're offering into something that the person wants. Then you're back in charge.

When I arrived at the factory, I knew that our position was compromised. For this meeting I needed all the guts, determination, and everything else I could muster—the future of Elizabeth Grant was at stake, and Elizabeth Grant was my life. I'm not going to pretend that this was easy or that I wasn't nervous—but I did it. We made an agreement that he would continue to supply us for a further six months on a cash and carry basis. Armed with this, I arranged a mass mailing to our clients and overnight re-established EG as a mail-order business.

As the business grew, I diversified. I started designing clothes and jewelry and opened an Elizabeth Grant Boutique. Initially I had a very small clientele, which grew through word of mouth. It was very successful and probably the only boutique I know of that introduced a range on Friday and by

Monday was sold out. One winter I went searching for white fabrics and found nothing because of the season. So I looked to another source and used finely brushed terry instead. I am fairly certain I broke the rules first about wearing winter white. In fact, I think I invented it.

Whatever I made from the boutique I kept in my own account. This became my nest egg—my security—a guarantee for my future.

As a result of these Herculean efforts, I now enjoyed every material advantage—even a chauffeur named Albert—and could have eventually chosen to become a "lady who lunched." But this was not me. I was restless, easily bored, and eager to meet new people and rise to fresh challenges. There was no mistaking my achievements—my beauty empire was a huge success. My wealth was the result of years of dedication

Looking back I know that what saved us was my determination not to give up. I had learned, from my mother, the importance of making a plan. It's only when you don't have a plan that you run out of options. I also learned how important it is to understand every aspect of business and be self-reliant. Ultimately the buck always stops with you, making everything your responsibility.

Sydney and Elizabeth celebrating 1ˢᵗ Anniversary

Elizabeth and Sydney night-clubbing

Elizabeth in Cannes

Sydney dressed for golf

CHAPTER 10

A GOOD MARRIAGE IS A PARTNERSHIP OF TWO PEOPLE
1948–1990

New marriages require a period of adjustment. In my case, it was I who did most of the adjusting and Sydney who expected it. I took this in my stride and made allowances for his set ways.

We settled into a flat, and like most people, took on hired help—one woman did the cooking, and one looked after the boys while I worked. And working is what I did, day and night. Don't forget, I had been in this habit since the age of thirteen and this didn't bother me!

In many ways, life with Sydney was like living with a stern headmaster. His problem was his heightened sense of superiority. He looked down on his fellow man. He thought no one met his level. He lectured friends, family, and me on how we should live and why those around us were wrong. He was very verbose and pedantic. At first I thought he was very clever and learned a great deal from him. After a while I found this rather pompous and irritating. As time went on and I grew more confident in my own opinions, I'd drive him crazy when I'd rear back at something he was saying and question it. He'd get terribly upset, and then I'd say, "Now hold on, Daphne, don't get your knickers in an uproar." I called him Daphne very often.

Sydney was very stubborn, very set in his ways. He was decidedly from the "old school," which believed the man rules the house.

I enjoyed cooking when I was home, and still do. One day, I served him Vichyssoise, and he complained, "The soup is cold."

"It's supposed to be cold!" I explained.

He pushed the plate away and very disparagingly said, "Don't serve me cold soup again."

He liked peas and hated onions. Once he found onions with his meat and I thought he'd faint dead away. "When I want other vegetables on my plate, I'll tell you," he said rather imperiously. And then there was the time I served a lovely side of batter-dipped, sautéed banana. He said, "I like dessert when I finish my entree. Honestly!"

Sydney always wore a shirt and tie—even on Sunday. While his fine sense of dressing is what had attracted me to him in the first place, this wonderful sense of élan and well-tailored made-to-measure suits, the very best shirts and leather shoes and Italian silk ties—I found that this was starting to irritate me. But he wasn't going to change, and I grew used to this oddity. I still loved his is meticulous attire, his intelligent brown eyes and melodious voice that had drawn me to him.

What I couldn't quite be sure of was how he really felt about me. I provided the effervescence of youth and charm. I was the go-getter, the raconteur and humorist, the honey that attracted bees. At public gatherings, Sydney often said, "I tell them the one about …"My problem was that I didn't believe I was attractive, even though I was. Certainly Sydney never told me I looked good, commented on my hair, nor did I ever see him look at me and smile with admiration. He never told me that he loved me, although he did call me darling all the time. I took this as "Just being Sydney" and only much later in life realized how this negatively impacted on my self-esteem. Many times business acquaintances pointed out how

I was not only attractive, but smart, talented, and "the whole package"—but I could never accept this as a compliment and instead questioned their motive. One Sunday I was walking down the street, dressed in a tight black skirt, wearing high black patent heels. My jacket was black-and-white checked and had a black patent belt with a thin line of red on the sides. A car pulled up, Engelbert Humperdinck popped his head out the window and said, "Some girls have got a little; some girls have some more. Kid, you've got it all from top to toe!" He drove away, and I stood there with my mouth open. Later when I told Sydney, he muttered something about, "Irresponsible musicians. What do they know?"

A mutual friend, playwright Adam Leslie, approached me with the idea of casting me in his upcoming show in Johannesburg. I was so excited at the prospect. I would have loved to be on the stage, but Sydney disparagingly remarked, "Local theater? Are you mad? Don't be ridiculous!" and that was the end of that.

I had always thought I'd like to have six children, but it wasn't to be. Soon after Paul was born I got pregnant again but miscarried. In thinking about this now, I have to concede that having many children was probably not in anyone's best interests. My sons love me and I love them dearly, but I don't think I was a very good mother to them. I was forever working and wrapped up in Elizabeth Grant when they were very little. And I suffered terrible migraines, something I had not experienced before my marriage. The migraines, however, were absolutely vicious and forced me into bed, sometimes for as long as three days. I still suffer them and have to be very careful about fragrances.

One year the boys wanted to give me a birthday present. They pooled their money and bought a large bottle of cheap cologne from a local drug store. I thanked them very sincerely, and I suppose I should have left it at that, but I thought it was the right opportunity to tell them never to settle for anything but the very best quality, even if it meant they'd have to save for a long time to buy it. I think they took it to heart because today, all my sons value things of excellence because they know they are well made and will last.

I, in the prime of life, bore no resemblance to the waif I had once been—emaciated, malnourished, physically abused, and emotionally neglected. My elaborate armor, magnificent in its complexity and design, masked the extensive network of my childhood scars. There was no balm of Torricelumn™ for my psyche; humor and self-imposed regimes of hard work were my reliable safety nets.

I continued to behave as I always had. In a way I lived a double life. Not even my closest friends had any idea about what I gone through or to what degree I had been degraded and humiliated.

Time and distance had plucked me from garish, ill-fitting hand-me-downs and set me into a delightful panoply of innovative fashion. Now I enjoyed an extensive wardrobe. Many of my day frocks and evening gowns were sewn by my personal couturier, often from my own designs. As with most fashionable women of the 1960s and '70s, mink caressed my shoulders in cold and inclement weather. And icons, Chanel and Dior, were part of my private dressing room's vocabulary.

When we married, I had no way of knowing I'd be with Sydney for over forty years. How can anyone predict the future? He was a devoted husband in his way. But at times, as in most marriages, it was a living hell, and the way I dealt with it was to immerse myself in work and just get on with life.

And what a life it was—intensive work, entertainment, and travel. We had a wide circle of fascinating friends, partied routinely, and every December flew off on holiday with the children to faraway destinations. We toured China, Japan, and Europe. I adored Rome.

We spent some time in France, too. I think we were on the Riviera when I spotted someone at a nearby table who I thought I knew very well. I sauntered over and said, "Hallo, darling! How are you? How's the family?" I didn't know her from Adam, but she was polite, sweet, and responded in kind. When I went back to the table Sydney said to me, "I didn't know you knew Claudette Colbert." What a surprise! I had been speaking to Claudette Colbert! With a twinkle in my eye, I replied, "Was that Claudette Colbert? Mm—I thought I knew her ..." and we both laughed.

I had no use, really, for Monaco with all its gambling casinos filled with mucky-mucks. And Paris was beautiful to look at, but because I didn't speak French, as lovely as it was, I didn't feel welcome there.

One of our earliest trips was to Hollywood. I really wanted to visit America, experience it for myself. And you know, in the early '60s, Hollywood and Vine were already going to seed. The streets were dirty, not really as glamorous as I thought they'd be. But I enjoyed touring the studios; they were still very busy. During that visit, I saw Marilyn Monroe. I have to tell you, she was a beautiful girl. Her skin glowed. She looked incandescent, as though lit from within—truly beautiful.

In addition to our regular trips, we went to London to check on business, visit friends and family. And for me, it was also about shopping. I could live in Harrods! On one of my flights to London, I wore nothing but a slip under my mink coat and luxuriated in the experience. Of course, I was travelling light deliberately; I was planning to stuff my luggage with all the items I wanted to bring back.

I'm not entirely sure when the Buckingham Palace visit took place. But what happened was, I was having my hair done and while I was sitting in my chair, someone leaned over to me and pointed out the lady-in-waiting to Queen Elizabeth. Ladies-in-waiting are always titled aristocrats.

Well, not wanting to miss an opportunity, I went over to her, introduced myself, and we chatted for a bit. I told her how much I loved seeing the Windsor's waving from that famous balcony on numerous occasions, and that I had always wondered about the room located behind it.

"Why not come to tea?" she suggested. "You can see the room, then."

I thanked her, gave her my card, and an invitation arrived soon after. I was thrilled! Off I went, not really expecting to meet the Queen, but still … and did you know, they have a secret entrance on the side? I suppose it's the tradesmen's entrance. That's how they admitted me. I was escorted to the very room I had been so curious about. The lady-in-waiting and I were served tea, and it was delightful. The room itself was not very large or quite as imposing as I thought it would be—nicely appointed, though. After all, it *is* in a palace. Still, as I drank my tea, I thought, well, this is no different from the tea I drink at home, and I told her so. We laughed.

Having a grand time with luminaries is fun, but I have always said, it doesn't matter where you come from or where you start, it only matters where you end up, how you inform yourself, how you conduct yourself. That's what makes you a good person.

A family friend was married to a successful theatrical agent who listed Danny Kaye, the Nicholas Brothers, Tony Martin, and Cyd Charisse as his clients, among many others. Sydney and I enjoyed a memorable dinner with husband-and-wife, Martin and Charisse. When we met them, I was struck by the passage of time, although both had aged gracefully. They were truly genuine, delightful people. I think Cyd Charisse's legs are the most beautiful I've seen. Hers and Marlene Dietrich's—absolutely stunning. You know, when Cyd died recently, I was disappointed that media coverage was so sparse. She was a Hollywood legend.

On the last Saturday of each and every month, Sydney and I hosted a party. We drew up the guest list in the same order of importance each time, always putting the bank manager and his wife first.

In fact, it was I who arranged things and ensured their success. I was the glue in my marriage and my world.

I was in charge of preparing the buffets, and I cooked most of the food. The parties had food themes. Sometimes it was a curry theme, or maybe Chinese, or stroganoff. I remember the fun we had with an "all balls" evening; every item on the table was some kind of ball or other.

Everyone knew about the parties as their reputation grew, and I can honestly say they were always successful. I provided the jokes and entertainment. And if Ann was with me, we enjoyed doing a variety of comedy skits and spoofs. I loved the spotlight. I naturally gravitated toward it, and I kept people in stitches.

I really do enjoy cooking and baking. One lovely afternoon I decided to bake a cake. Now, I am my mother's daughter in so many ways—I insist on a scrupulously clean kitchen. So there I was busying myself with flour and butter and whatnot, when I suddenly spotted a very large bluebottle fly on my spotless floor. Flies breed disease. Flies have no place in a kitchen. So I found a newspaper, rolled it up, and quickly as I could, smashed that fly. But it didn't budge. It didn't flutter, it hadn't squashed. I hit it again. Nothing. I was getting frustrated. I just batted away at the bloody thing until finally, on closer inspection, I realized I had murdered a very plump currant!

Once I managed to poison an entire Japanese delegation—fourteen or maybe sixteen people, I think.

It started out with the very best of intentions. This took place in the '70s. Harry Nishigushi was a good friend. He had his offices in the same building as we did, and he often joined Sydney at the golf course.

One November he walked in to my office looking very glum to say he was being recalled to Japan and had to begin selling off his office equipment and the like, and he was very disappointed because he'd hoped to spend Christmas in Johannesburg. So I said, "Well, come to me for dinner on November 24. It's pretty close to Christmas, anyhow, and we'll simply pretend it is.

Cheer up! He soon brightened and asked if it might be possible to include the vice-consul and his wife and a few other delegates. I said the more the merrier and it was all set.I worked out a good list of my own friends to add to his and ended up with a large group. I planned carefully. I used Chinese bowls and had Japanese flower arrangements, and for the buffet, I decided to blend an interesting assortment. I ordered four large chickens, removed the gizzards, the giblets, and all of that, and made a really good chicken broth to serve with noodles. Sounds good, right? And the kitchen staff roasted all the chickens. We cut them in attractive pieces, and I served them atop a large bed of vegetables, along with rice with mushrooms, peas, and peppers.For dessert I made a huge Christmas cake, which I served with warm vanilla custard.

What a success it was! The Japanese loved the food—Harry had at least three helpings. When they left, there was much bowing and smiling—everyone obviously enjoyed themselves. Sydney and I went to bed, exhausted, and then I woke with terrible cramps, nausea, the whole bit. I was violently ill, and as sick as I was, Sydney was even sicker. "We're dying," he moaned. "Must have been your cooking."

I think the culprits were the chicken livers. I really don't know for sure. But something tells me it was the chicken and probably salmonella poisoning.

Well, the next day, when I managed to struggle out of bed, I began calling all my friends to see if they'd enjoyed themselves. One after the other told me how sick they were; a few thought they'd caught some flu before they arrived. There was no answer at one of the homes—I figure they must have gone to hospital. I called my dear friend Stella and her husband answered. "She's very ill," he said. "The doctor's with her now." I listened, terrified, and for the moment, said nothing. How was I going to face the Japanese delegation? Everyone in my immediate circle had succumbed. I didn't know what to do about poor Harry. You won't believe this, but when I finally did speak to him, he was fine. In fact, all of the Japanese were fine. Only my friends and family got sick. How or why this was the case, I have no idea. Yes ... it is possible they lied out of politeness, but I don't think so, I really don't.

When the boys were still young and at home, I discovered a lump in my breast. I found it one morning after I stepped out of the shower. Terrified isn't even close to what I was feeling. I sought attention immediately and met a surgeon. He wanted me in the hospital right away.

I didn't want to frighten the boys, so I didn't tell them a thing. I simply checked into the hospital and prayed. A few hours before they wheeled me into the operating room, when no one was around, I took a lipstick out of my handbag and drew a huge X on my breast, because I was so worried they'd make a mistake. I'd heard a lot of horror stories ... well, hasn't everyone?

When I came to, I was staring into the surgeon's face. In those days, when a woman had breast cancer, they didn't wake her up after a biopsy and inform her they were going to remove the breast or the nodes, or whatever—they just went ahead and did whatever was necessary. So, as soon as I was awake, I realized my chest was flattened and bound, and I was almost too afraid to ask, but of course, I absolutely had to know. So I said, "Tell me ... do I still have ... ?"

"Yes, Elizabeth." He smiled. "It's still there. The lump was benign."

I was so relieved that I didn't realize he was trying to be stern with me.

"Elizabeth, do you have any idea what you did? Do you know how hard it is to remove a huge swath of greasy lipstick and thoroughly sterilize a field?"

"Doctor," I said, trying to ignore his scolding, "I really hate your tie ..." He stared at me, eyes crinkling, and then walked away and came back with a scissors. He promptly cut off his tie. "Happy now?"

We became fast friends.

My life, restored to normal once more, was back to work and soon arranging for the boys to go off to various boarding schools for a proper English-style education, although Darryl only went for about six months, as he really was unhappy. So we brought him home.

I was in touch with my mother, who regularly came over for a visit until Isaac died. My younger sister, Lynn, had married a Scottish VIP. She is ten years younger than I, and I wasn't around when she was growing up. I hardly knew her. It's only in these last few years, since Ann's death, that we've become very close.

As for Ann, she had married her second husband, Sam, and had another son. We formed quite a pair. We loved making harmless mischief. We'd play practical jokes for our own amusement. For instance, we'd walk into a crowded elevator, ostensibly as two strangers, and then make a small scene, tossing barbs at each other while onlookers wondered how soon they could escape us. Finally, Ann, the "straight man," would say to me, "I didn't come here to be insulted!" And I'd quip, "Really? Where do you normally go?" Then we'd leave the elevator. Straight out of Groucho Marx.

We also walked into the waiting room of our dentist or doctor, picked up the dog-eared magazines, and flipped through them.

"Oh my, have you seen this?" I asked Ann. "The Titanic sank!"

"Are you serious? That's just horrible!"

A moment later, Ann exclaimed, "My God! Queen Victoria has died!"

"All right, all right, ladies," the receptionist chimed in. "We're due to get some new reading material shortly."

Ann and I had been through so much together. She protected me when I was a child, and I know she would have taken a bullet for me if the occasion ever arose. But, as with so many sisters, we had a falling out about something so trivial when I think about it now. I mean, no matter how horrible it was, it really wasn't life shattering. But you wouldn't have convinced me or her of this back then. We were both very stubborn and dug in our heels. So we stopped talking to each other, and we didn't see each other for an extremely long time. I suppose at one point I thought we were finished for good.

And then one afternoon, around lunchtime, Darryl, who was a grown man by now, took a call from the switchboard in our offices and told me that that Sam (Ann's husband) was on the phone. Sam said Ann was desperately ill in hospital.

"I'll be right there," I told him. I had a miniature dachshund, Sadie, who went everywhere with me, and I scooped her up, threw on my mink, and raced to the hospital. I knew dogs weren't permitted, so I was very careful to hide Sadie in my coat. I hadn't seen Ann in ages, but it didn't matter. She was ill. I was her sister. She needed me, and I needed her. Well, as soon as she saw me, her eyes widened, and before she could say a word, Sadie's tiny face popped out from the folds in my coat, and I put a silencing finger to my lips and whispered to Ann, "Shh."

The bed began to shake. "Don't make me laugh, it hurts," were the first words Ann uttered. She looked like hell, but apart from her illness, it was like no time had passed at all. I was so relieved we patched things up, and later, when she was fully recovered, we formed a new bond with new rules, and that was that. We hadn't spoken for ten years, and in hindsight I regret this because those ten years could never be recaptured. Time past is time gone, and time speeds by so quickly.

Time. How to capture its meaning? Where does a life go? I have no idea. I arrived in South Africa in 1948 and stayed until the 1990s. In those decades I struggled, rose to success, lost everything, made it again, watched three sons grow to manhood, and worked within the frame of a difficult marriage.

Rodney married and eventually left for Canada and settled in Toronto. Today he is a well-known hair color technician with a staggering client load. Darryl worked at Elizabeth Grant, and then he established his own successful acrylic company. Paul also worked at Elizabeth Grant until he had a huge row with Sydney and left. He started a management training company and moved to Toronto without healing the rift. I felt a great loss. He stayed in touch with Darryl, and Darryl gave me all his latest news. A mother needs to be in contact with her children, and this was a sad time in my life.

Another lesson learned only too late—there is no point in not speaking. By having no dialogue nothing happens. You remain stuck without the ability to go forward.

The seasons flowed one into the other ... and "to everything, a purpose under heaven."

I was always full of energy, healthy, and vigorous. I didn't look, act, think, move, walk, or talk like other people my own age. My face, thanks to my Torricelumn™, still looked good. And though my hair was graying, it shone with bright silver and bloomed into a remarkable halo of dazzling white. No matter what the calendar said, I remained youthful. My motto has always been, *'Age is just another number.'* It isn't about how old I am; it's the way I feel.

Sydney became very ill, moaning in pain as he moved about the house. He was so Teutonic about everything. He was strict, stoic, and harsh. To admit to being ill was not in his vocabulary, and he would not allow me to call the doctor. We argued about this until I gave up and just tried to be there for him. One day, he came to me asking for a needle and thread—he wanted to tighten the band in his underpants. I decided I had to know what he weighed, so I commented on how I needed to go on a diet—how we both had said we needed to lose weight, and I managed to convince him to get on the scale. From that point on, I watched him slowly waste away.

He was skin and bones and yellow, but he still refused to get help. He wasn't going back to any "damn hospital." I called our doctor friend and suggested he come for a visit on a pretext of just popping in to say hello.

Sydney was too weak to protest anything. He was admitted to the cancer ward, where they made him as comfortable as possible. I was no longer in a state of denial and realized that it was now a matter of time. Now I spent my days nursing Sydney, but it was becoming increasingly difficult, and I was losing sleep and not eating. I was a wreck, and I lost a lot of weight. I felt vulnerable, terrified, and so weary. I remember how, at one point, when I was visiting him, I was so overwhelmed, I just collapsed.

It wasn't long after that when the doctors said there was nothing more they could do for him—he had to go home. And then I just picked up the phone and called Paul. All I said was, "Paul … it's time …" and he quickly interjected, "I'm on my way, Mum."

I don't know what I would have done were it not for Paul. He arrived, and he took complete charge. He nursed and bathed his father. He stayed at his bed reading and talking to him while he was awake. He urged me to rest.

Death was imminent. Paul arranged for hospice care. By now Sydney was out of consciousness most of the time. The hospice nurse took Paul aside and said, "Try to keep reassuring him to just let go." On the last day he woke up and asked Paul, "Promise me that you will take care of Mummy."

That night hospice called to say that Sydney had passed.

We held a service for him the following day—he was cremated. And that was that. Paul left soon after to return home, and before he went, I took hold of him and said, "I just want you to know that as far as I'm concerned, whatever happened in the past ... well, the slate is wiped clean."

Paul's love and compassion had touched me profoundly. It still does.

All I remember feeling at the time of Sydney's death was numb. I didn't cry; I hardly knew what I was thinking, only that two sensations flooded me at the same time. First, I felt overwhelmed with relief—the suffering was over. The second emotion I recall was pure bewilderment. I had absolutely no idea what I was supposed to do, what I wanted to do, or what needed to be done. I who had become so independent felt lost.

CHAPTER 11

EIGHTY IS JUST
ANOTHER NUMBER

As I recount these events, I realize that I didn't have time for bereavement. Widowhood, while officially conferred upon me, seems somehow misplaced. Rather, I was once more a pioneer finding myself at the end of one journey and about to explore another. The contradiction in my relationship with Sydney was that even though he had forced me into total spousal dependence, I remained a determined and independent woman. A brief glimpse into my feelings about losing him lies in his wardrobe. For two years I did not disturb his clothes. Whatever bond I'd had with him, my opinions and conclusions shifted over time. People who knew Sydney, tell me he loved me. I didn't feel that when he was alive. Now, I can see their point.

As to getting on with life, I met surprises. As breathtakingly beautiful as South Africa is, it was never a country I felt I belonged to. I was a Londoner by birth, and to a great degree, by disposition. I was an ex-pat who had fled the misery of the Second World War. So, whenever racial politics and violence roared around me, I felt like a fish out of water. And I still had family there—Ann lived a few floors above me, and Darryl and Gill were settled in Johannesburg, as well.

Business continued as usual for two years amidst stories circulating about high crime, unrest, and growing tensions.

I knew quite a few people who had been mugged. One of my friends seemed to take it in her stride, saying she was a "tough old bird" and would be okay, but I am not that kind of person. Don't forget, I was an old lady living alone, and I began to feel vulnerable. I remember dashing off in the early morning to run errands and then curling up in my flat come noontime. I felt safer that way. I locked all the doors, front and back. But I also felt like I had imprisoned myself. I love to take baths. I do my best thinking in the tub. Well, I talk to my father every day while I'm sorting out various problems. I think he points me in the right direction or actually intervenes on my behalf. Our bathroom was lined in mirrors, floor to ceiling. One evening, just as I stepped out—actually, only one foot was out—they came crashing down and shattered in the tub. I could have been cut to ribbons, but I missed it by a fraction. Once again I knew my father was looking after me.

Something even more frightful occurred sometime after Sydney's death. I was sitting in my favorite chair, watching television, as I always did in the evenings. I must have shut it off about midnight and gone to bed. The next morning, I saw was a bullet hole in the window facing the chair. There was broken glass everywhere. Terrified, I called the police. Well, when the police arrived and surveyed the damage, they found the bullet lodged into the headrest of the very chair I had been sitting in. If I had been there past midnight, the bullet would have struck me in the face.

I couldn't believe any of it. Neither could the police. No forced entry, and my flat was on the fourth floor overlooking the garden, the pool, and beyond that, the walkway. The police figured the bullet had ricocheted from somewhere. All I knew was I was scared out of my wits and that once again my Papa had saved me.

Paul and I talked to each other fairly often; one night he called around midnight, and I told him about the kinds of violence and crime going on, including my own brush with it. Well, Paul exclaimed, "Why don't you come here? Pack up and come to Canada! You'll feel free and safe here!" Without a hesitation, I said I'd go if Rodney also thought it would be okay, as I had no intention of imposing myself on my children. We talked for a few more minutes, rang off, and the phone rang again almost immediately. I thought it was Paul, but it was Rodney, and like a dumb cluck, I started prattling on about how I had just been talking about him, and what a coincidence ... "No, Mum," he said, "you don't understand. Paul just called me. I'm phoning to tell you to come as quickly as you can."

Ann wasn't happy. She begged me to stay on, to move to Cape Town with her, but she got nowhere. I had never been to Canada. I, in my mid seventies, was still an adventurer. Besides, I had not yet met Paul's wife, Marion, and *their* children. An entire flock was waiting in the wings to greet me. Canada, by all accounts, was a good place to live, despite its reputed harsh climate.

Economically, it was sound. Politically and socially, it was diverse and pluralistic. Whatever I might have felt about this northern dominion, I'd have to decide sooner rather than later. If not now, when?

I moved with the speed of light. There was much to do. I rolled up my sleeves and went straight to work. I dismantled the business, the offices. I sold the film studio, the sophisticated cameras, and other related equipment. Next, I sold off enormous quantities of warehouse stock. In no small measure, this amounted to a tidy fortune.

I informed Agnes, my housekeeper for decades, that the entire contents of my condo were up for sale. Agnes passed the word on, and in one day, Agnes managed to sell everything and anything that wasn't nailed down or restricted for further use by me. Agnes was a marvel.

I called my real estate agent and told him I was selling my home. I closed the sale with the first couple who arrived. Then, I sold Sydney's car. I had to deal with insurance, taxes, a million forms; I had to get certain clearances. A lawyer friend—thank God for him!—was able to get me through most of the hoops. It wasn't easy. For instance, you couldn't just up and leave South Africa, with any degree of money. I entrusted him to look after that end of things, which he did. Over the course of two years, money came to me in dribs and drabs until all of it arrived.

It took me three weeks to pack up, sell up, and finalize everything. Even I was amazed. I phoned Paul. No one was home, so I left a message. I said, "Please call me—it's urgent." I finished a few errands, returned home, and later, Paul phoned and I floored him with the news that I was all ready to leave.

At his suggestion, I flew to London and met him there. Great idea and great fun. Emotionally, it was good to have him to lean on, and I appreciated my escort. It was our first real quality time ever spent together. We shopped, walked, ate, and laughed a lot.

Canada did not disappoint me; my family was more charming than I could have imagined. I settled into a small and suitable flat and immediately immersed myself in the new culture.

Sydney had always told me there was a great deal of wisdom in doing this. When he first arrived in Johannesburg in the 1930s, he spent quite some time poking about everywhere, getting the lay of the land, as it were, before settling down. I found there is much sense in this. I paid a great deal of attention to Canadians; I wanted to know what they liked, where and how they shopped, what they ate, what they disliked, and how they expressed themselves.

To keep myself occupied I wrote copious letters. I had always been a prolific writer. One letter in particular took the form of a complaint to Queen I. "I am horribly disappointed with my new passport. It is ugly—maroon, orangey brown—god-awful! This isn't the British passport I recognize. It lacks grace. There are no vestiges of the Britain I once knew."

I received a very polite letter from the Buckingham Palace, which advised me that this was not their domain and handed direct my query to the customs office for the correct handling of such matters. The queen, alas, could do nothing about it. Then, I heard from the proper bureaucrats, who told me the new passport had to be thinner and in keeping with the new computerized and digitalized requirements. I replied that I appreciated this information, but what had this to do with the ugly cover?

I wrote a congratulatory letter to President Clinton when he first became president and received a signed, warm note of thanks.

One can always expect the unexpected from me. One of my favorite hobbies is rewriting the existing lyrics of well-known standards.

A few years ago, I needed an operation on my hand and was directed to a doctor who specialized in hand and breast surgery. I thought this a bit odd and asked him what made him specialize in these two areas. He smiled and replied, "While I'm sure everyone wonders about this, very few patients actually ask me." I love doctors but hate injections. The treatment was injecting a needle into my finger. Even though it was admittedly a small surgical procedure, I was very nervous about it. So I wrote new lyrics to the classic Bob Hope signature song, "Thanks for the Memories." Then, when I was lying down with my arm stuck through a small curtain and couldn't see what the doctor was doing—thank God!—I felt the needle when he froze my hand. A nurse was standing next to me, taking my pulse. It was racing. My blood pressure was high too. I said to the doctor, "Listen, I've written a song for you" and I started to sing:

Thanks for the *mammaries* …
I was size thirty-two,
And now my thanks to you,
I have a date,
I stay out late,
And it's all due to you …
So thank you so much …

Thanks for the *mammaries* …
No padding is required,
My date is never hired,
And all the money that I paid,
I finished up by getting laid …
So thank you so much.

People who see me can't believe it.
They think that I've been putting on some weight.
But when they see me wearing nothing,
They know it's true—
My thanks to you, oh,

Thanks for the *mammaries*,
I'm getting married soon,
I'll go on honeymoon,
And you're invited to my home,
I hope to see you soon …
So thank you … so much!

Of course the nurse was hysterical ... but she said, "You have to stop singing now because you're making him laugh and your hand's cut open." I shut up immediately.

Part of my cultural immersion involved participation in seniors' group activities. I helped with fundraising events. I wrote and produced plays, naughty plays, like the one about Snow White, a notorious cocaine dealer aided by seven accomplices.

With the passage of time, I decided I wanted to become a citizen. I am a very proud Canadian. I love this country—and I have never been happier.

I visited the nearby mall, read extensively, gave public lectures to women's groups—and generally kept busy, but the family noticed I was lagging a bit, like a race horse trying to get up a head of steam but finding myself jerking at the bit. One day Marion approached me with a suggestion—did I want to get Elizabeth Grant going once more, in Canada? What a question!

The idea resounded with the sharp snap of a starting pistol—yes! I was first out of the gate. I was over the moon—nothing could have been more wonderful. Here I was, not middle aged, but old and about to start a business again.

I once gave a lecture and I started it by saying, "If I applied for a job and said, 'I am in my eighties. I'm deaf. I can't drive. I don't know how to use a computer, and I can't answer a cell phone,' would you employ me? This is an interesting point."

I told Marion we had to make out a list—the who, the what, the when, and the how, and we did it again. We formed a partnership and step by step forged ahead. She is an absolute marvel, and together we have started to recreate an empire.

We got things ready, and headed to The Shopping Channel in Mississauga. I had been watching it for a long time, and we both agreed that it was an excellent outlet that would allow me to reach Canadian women and men simultaneously across the country without all the headaches of the retail trade, not to mention the overhead, the constant travel, and the hundreds of employees needing training.

I figured I had nothing to lose by attempting that route first. It just seemed like a perfect match for me. In my entire career, I had never needed advertising—Elizabeth Grant, the company, always flourished because of word of mouth.

The buyer at the Shopping Channel recognized in me a remarkable charisma and a genuine sincerity in my words. She saw the vast potential of my products, placed an order, and booked me for three half-hour shows. I was elated by the ease at which things fell into place. Perhaps I knew even then that this was going to be a match made in heaven. And it was.

On Wednesday, August 5, 1998, I walked into the studio for the first time, faced the camera knowingly, and said, "Hi everybody. My name is Elizabeth Grant. You don't know me from a bar of soap, but I am going to change your life."

And I did.

Elizabeth outside office in Navy suit with Herman

Elizabeth outside the office with Herman
and Pepe who came to the office every day
– I called them "my co-directors"

Elizabeth with good friend Israeli Prime Minister, Rabin

My beloved Romey

Elizabeth in Florida with Herman #2

CHAPTER 12

HERE'S TO LIFE—AN INFINITE REALM OF POSSIBILITIES

Of course, the story is not over. In the years since 1998, the company has gone international. Our products are reaching millions in Canada, the United States, England, South Africa, Germany, Russia, and beyond. The success of the business makes me proud. Who would have thought it could happen again?

I wanted to go back to England, and at the right time, Marion looked at me and said, "Why not?" We hopped on a plane. Our marketing strategy—Elizabeth Grant Comes Home!

Today, Elizabeth Grant is so inundated with product demand that we may have to once again increase the size of the premises. At The Shopping Channel in Canada, I draw the largest audience and sell more products than anyone else—and always with my trademark humour and charm. I have won two "Shoppys" in a row, akin to the "People's Choice Awards" for outstanding product and popularity. On December 4, 2009, I received a Lifetime Achievement Award from The Wifts Foundation in Los Angeles, California.

I am proud of these accolades, but that's not where the true satisfaction lies for me … it's in making people happy, helping women turn back the clock, helping women realize everyone can attain their dreams. Just because we grow old doesn't mean that we lose our voice or stop dreaming.

Sometimes I wonder what Isaac would say if he could see me now. But then I say to myself, had I not had that childhood I believe I would not be what I am today, and that's self-assured, confident, and happy at last.

I hope whosoever is reading this will know that it's up to you. I truly believe you can be and do whatever you want to be. But you have to want it so much you can almost taste it. It's a question of moving forward and believing in your true feelings. Let nobody tell you what you should be or what you should do. By all means listen to your peers, but in the end, do what's in your heart.

I'm having an absolute ball! I am in my late eighties. It just goes to show you that you never know.

I often laugh at myself: "I'm as deaf as a loaf of bread." As to my mortality, I say, "I'm on the short list."

I have never been happier that I am here in Canada. I feel I am alive.

So here I am in the autumn of my life (what autumn? That's gone—it's actually the winter of my life) and I think to myself, *Mmmmmmm, why don't I have a talk show?* It would be fun, and I certainly can dish out advice on almost anything and at the same time make you feel comfortable and make you laugh. Am I a bit nuts? If I could have chosen another career, it would have been hosting a television show; in fact, I'm still considering it. Maybe—it certainly can't hurt.

Sometimes I talk about opening an Elizabeth Grant Spa. I talk as though I am on the threshold of my life—I can't help it. I walk around with spring in my heart in the autumn of my life.

Like chicken soup, it's very good for you.

Regardless of the season, my world is sunny. My story illustrates the infinite realm of possibilities. Here's to life!